Modern Scandinavian
Literature in Translation
MSLT

Editor: Robert E. Bjork,
Arizona State University

Board Members:
Evelyn Firchow,
University of Minnesota
Niels Ingwersen,
University of Wisconsin
Torborg Lundell,
University of California
at Santa Barbara
Patricia McFate,
The American-
Scandinavian
Foundation
Harald S. Naess,
University of Wisconsin
Sven H. Rossel,
University of Washington
Paul Schach,
University of
Nebraska–Lincoln
George C. Schoolfield,
Yale University
Ross Shideler,
University of California
at Los Angeles

Land
of
Wooden
Gods

Jan Fridegård

Trägudars land
Volume 1 in the Holme Trilogy
Translated, with an afterword
and notes, by Robert E. Bjork
University of Nebraska Press
Lincoln and London

Originally published
as *Trägudars land*
in *Trilogin om*
trälen Holme,
copyright © 1940 by
Aase and Stefan Fridegård
Translation, notes, and
afterword copyright
© 1989 by Robert E. Bjork
Library of Congress
Cataloging-in-Publication Data
Fridegård, Jan, 1897–1968.
[Trägudars land. English]
Land of wooden gods /
by Jan Fridegård ;
translated, with
an afterword and notes,
by Robert E. Bjork. p. cm.
–(Modern Scandinavian
literature in translation)
Translation of: Trägudars
land. "Volume 1 in the
Holme trilogy."
Bibliography: p.
ISBN 0-8032-1970-9
(alk. paper)
6870-x (pbk.)
I. Title   II. Series
PT9875.F788T6713 1989
839.7'372 – dc19
89-5275 CIP

I am deeply grateful to Steven C. Spronz, Esq.,
without whose timely and generous help
this translation would not have been published.

Robert E. Bjork

Contents

Land
of
Wooden
Gods

The settlement was well hidden among the fir trees, and anyone traveling along the cove down below had to know it was there already to notice it. Yet from inside the biggest of the log houses you had a clear view across the lake through a couple of openings in the south wall. A huge refuse pile stood by one of the longer walls, visited by dogs, ants, and flies. At night, when everything was quiet in the timbered halls and the smoke had stopped rising through the holes in the roofs, a sniffing wolf, a cautious fox, or a white-faced badger could grub for a minute in the pile while keeping watchful eyes on the dwellings.

About fifty yards from the main structure were two smaller

dwellings, along with a stable and a pigsty. Their timber rested directly on the ground, whereas the high hall stood on a stone foundation. In several places in the forest and on a slope by the lake, the earth was tilled in little patches where slender barley stalks, mixed with the tall, glistening grass, swayed in the light breezes moving among the blades. A number of footpaths began at the settlement and vanished in different directions through the trees. The most well-trodden path led to the lake.

Toward evening, the settlement's inhabitants came home from all directions. Indolent warriors with dangling swords, bows, or spears. Male and female thralls who, with cunning or uneasy glances at the high hall, went toward the two smaller dwellings, crawled in through a yard-high door, and disappeared. In one of the thralls' dwellings a baby started screaming, soon getting an even louder response from the main building.

Several thralls handed things in at the door of the main building: a string of fish, a hare, or a rough clump of bog ore. From a place a little distance into the forest the sound of hammer blows resounded all day long, and when they stopped, you could hear murmuring voices. The voices came from some thralls working at a smithy consisting of a metal wedge lodged between two protruding pieces of rock. They were forging tools and weapons.

In one of the smaller dwellings where the female thralls lived lay a figure who hadn't worked for a few days. She had fixed a bed for herself below her bench so she could rest better, and an older friend helped her when she gave birth. Someone would sneak in to her occasionally with some flowers or a handful of blueberries. Next to the straw bed was a bowl of roast fish. There was constant twilight in the dwelling, but just after noon, when the sun had started to sink, two shafts of light came in through the openings

4

on the south side and shot to the opposite wall. The beams climbed toward the ceiling and disappeared in about an hour.

The smell of summer and pine needles penetrated the female thralls' dwelling. The mother cried all evening, rocking the baby in her arms. When her friends came home, they kept an uneasy lookout on the high hall so they could give word when the time had come.

After the chieftain and the warriors had eaten their fill, they leaned back in their seats, grumbled among themselves, and sucked the beer from their beards. After a while, the chieftain motioned to a female thrall attending table, and she walked to the thralls' dwelling with the message. The mother rose to her knees and, with the baby clasped to her breast, cried still louder.

The door to the high hall stood open to the summer night. Six or seven warriors sat on each side of the long table, and behind them their black and gold shields hung in rows with the bows above them on wooden pegs. The hall was cordoned off behind the chieftain; he lived there with his family. The shrine of the gods, with its mute wooden figures, stood at the far end.

The warriors slept on their benches in the high hall. A few male thralls – who were overseers or very skillful workers – had permission to stay inside the door during meals or when the warriors were talking or wrestling at night.

As the mother came crawling out of the little dwelling with her baby clutched to her chest, the warriors and thralls leaned forward so they could see her through the door. She stopped twice on the path between the buildings. With tear-filled eyes she thought about running and looked toward the forest, but the stare of the wolf pack inside the hall froze her and pulled her on. If she ran they would spring to their feet and seize her before she could find a place to hide. A dog got up from the grass by the path, yawned, and followed sniffing after her for a few steps.

She climbed over the two logs that formed the doorstep, tried to wipe the tears away on her right shoulder, and walked forward to the chieftain. The light of the fire and the departing day blended together, enlarging the figures around her. She laid the baby down at the chieftain's feet and tried to read his expression through the darkness. All the warriors sat turned toward him now, motionless. You could have mistaken them for wooden statues if one or another didn't twitch his beard either in excitement or sympathy.

The baby had a piece of cloth wrapped around its stomach but otherwise was naked. It screwed up its face to start screaming but caught sight of the fire and blinked in surprise. It had black hair, and two of the warriors looked meaningfully first at each other, then at the mother's blond mane.

The chieftain sat silent and motionless, leaning his head in his hand and looking down at the child. His short, thick legs were crisscrossed with leather thongs, and his sword hilt was more beautiful than the other warriors'. His hairline began right above his eyebrows; his forehead was just a pair of red creases. His nose was thick, his beard brown. Like the other warriors' beards, his was darker around his mouth from food scraps and dirt. The mother stood before him, wringing her hands, not taking her eyes off his ugly face.

The thralls by the door, tired after the day's work, showed little interest in what was happening farther up in the hall. All but one. He crouched as if ready to spring, his head thrust forward and his eyes burning like explosive, menacing coals. He had broader cheekbones than the others, and two black, evenly clipped locks of hair fell down over them. Once the chieftain's eye wandered down among the thralls, and when he saw the dark warning in the thrall's face, his beard moved to reveal a contemptuous grin. A young woman looked out from the interior of the hall, troubled by the silence.

'Stor and Tan,' the chieftain called.

Two of the thralls down near the door got up and came forward. The chieftain pointed to the baby with his foot and said, 'Put the troll-child in the woods.'

Tan bent down quickly, grabbed the baby, and walked toward the door, followed by Stor. The mother ran after them crying loudly, but the warriors got up and stood like a wall between her and the thralls who walked off with the child. It struggled and screamed when they got outside the door as the chill night closed on its delicate limbs.

The woman inside the hall shuddered and went back to her own child, who lay on the bed. When Stor and Tan were gone, the black-haired thrall turned and looked at the chieftain, who smiled for the second time at his threat. The baby might have been allowed to live if he hadn't encountered such defiance in his thralls, he thought, yawning hugely.

As soon as Tan and Stor disappeared, two warriors started wrestling in the open area between the fire pit and the long table. The other warriors gathered in a ring around them, and the thralls tried to see between their legs. The childless mother went out, holding one arm in front of her face.

The warriors crashed to the floor, and no one saw the dark-haired thrall slip out. Only after a while, when the battle was decided, did the chieftain notice he was gone.

'Where's Holme?' he asked, but no one knew. 'Has he gone after Stor and Tan?' But the warriors answered that just a moment ago he'd been sitting in his place and wouldn't be able to find Stor and Tan after such a long time.

The chieftain went in to his wife, the warriors started yawning, a couple of female thralls arranged the benches for the night and then went to their dwelling. Two of the younger warriors talked quietly a while and then made off for the female thralls' dwelling. They stopped outside and softly called the names of a couple of the younger women. But no one came out that night; only the mother's sobs answered them from inside. From their dwelling, the male thralls were pleased to see the disappointed warriors returning to their beds.

Stor and Tan took long strides away from the settlement, Tan muttering peevishly about the baby's crying. When it wouldn't settle down, he held it to his chest with an embarrassed look at Stor and pulled part of his shirt up over it. The child quieted down and closed its eyes when it felt the warmth from the thrall's body, and Stor nodded approvingly.

Both men kept a silent lookout for a good place to abandon the child. They dreaded the moment when they would have to put it on the ground and walk away. They had carried a good many babies out but had always tried to find a place without ants. But what could they do about the sniffing muzzles and gleaming eyes that would soon approach stealthily through the trees? Or maybe the sun would find the child untouched when it came up and then keep it alive until the next night.

They laid the baby in the green moss on the south side of a large rock, still warm from the sun, and then hurried away. A songthrush was singing very close by, and you could faintly hear dogs barking in a distant settlement.

The mother heard their footsteps and wailed louder. When

they came in, they went to bed immediately, ignoring their companions' questions. They hadn't seen Holme and didn't care where he had gone.

Holme had run barefoot straight into the woods. He didn't know which way Stor and Tan had gone; they had different places where they left the babies and never used the same place twice. At first he ran haphazardly but soon felt resistance in his body and changed direction. That felt better, and he flew forward through the woods, silent as an owl.

He was standing behind a tree when Stor and Tan came walking home again. You could barely see the path they were following. Holme's teeth flashed, and he moved on in the direction from which they had come.

He saw visions that urged him forward. He imagined a wolf prowling around the baby, sniffing it, sinking its teeth into it, and carrying it off to a safer place to eat. He clenched his fists, longing to have the wolf's throat in them. Suddenly he slowed down and shifted direction slightly to the left.

In a small clearing in the forest he stopped again and listened. It was much brighter there; some light fell over the glade, although neither sun nor moon was out. Holme listened and retreated behind a tree trunk. He could hear snorting and twigs breaking on the other side of the glade.

A long, gray snout protruded from the brush, snorting and sniffing as the whole animal ventured out into the opening. Behind him came the other animals like a row of waddling, swaying blocks of stone. The wild boars followed closely in each other's tracks.

When the big lead boar was in the middle of the glade, it veered off, for some reason, directly to the left. The others followed, and soon the column of boars formed a right angle. All of them walked carefully out to where their leader had veered. A few half-grown animals trotted along at the rear. The bushes soon stopped moving as the last gray rump disappeared and the snorting died away. Holme gestured threateningly at the boars and rushed on like a shadow over the glade.

A nearly full-grown boar didn't find its way back to its herd until the next day. Where the herd had gone on in disarray in the forest, the boar had stumbled onto something strange. Soft and whimpering and smelling edible, it rolled away from his snout. The boar turned his head sideways, trying to tear the object with his left tusk. It slipped away again, waving its tiny paws. The boar lifted his head halfway, blinking and listening for the herd before continuing to investigate.

The boar had one of the tiny legs in its jaws when something came rushing up with a furious roar. The boar let go his hold and bolted away in a terrified wobbling gallop, making a hoarse, guttural noise with every bound.

Holme chased the boar a short distance but soon turned back panting and crouched down by the child. He turned it clumsily in his hands to see if it was hurt. Blood ran from one leg, and it screamed constantly. The severe creases in the father's face softened a little when he found that nothing serious had happened to the baby.

As Tan had done earlier, he held the child to his chest and folded part of his clothing over it. It whimpered for a while but eventually fell asleep from the warmth of its father's body and the swaying motion when he walked.

An hour's hasty walk brought him to a clearing, the middle of which was marshy and cold. He hopped on the tufts of grass, which rocked and sank under his weight. A white night mist hung brooding over the area. On the other side, the ground rose more steeply, and several giant pines that had climbed down the slope marked the beginning of the forest. The earth was tepid under them, and their trunks shone a warm red against the west where the sky still glowed.

Holme walked up the rise, turned around, and looked back at the marshy ground and the forest beyond it. He was far away from the settlement now. The rage had left his face, and those black eyes, which few had ever looked into, bore a grave, searching expression. He loosened his grip around the child and looked anxiously at it. As if sensing the father's gaze, it revealed its toothless gums and let out a closed-eyed howl.

Holme continued over the gravel ridge and soon came into a soft, dark spruce forest. Huge boulders overgrown with foot-deep moss lay there like gigantic sleeping animals. A large bird off among the trees took flight with a rumbling of wings.

He walked straight to where some jagged boulders formed a cairn that reached halfway to the tops of the trees. Apprehension filled his eyes and he mumbled an invocation or a promise of sacrifice. Even the song-thrushes had stopped their singing. It was the darkest moment in the summer night, and the silence made his hair stand on end.

Holme soon found the cave opening. The stone and the dry spruce branches lay as he had left them. The moss inside felt soft and dry as he crawled over it, supporting himself on one hand and both knees. With his other hand he pressed the child against him and groped about for the best place to lay it. The cave was cool and smelled of earth and roots. He thought for a moment before he laid the child down, then took off his garment and wound it several times around the baby. He positioned the infant as well as he could in the darkness and could feel that the little body was burning up. As he fumbled about to find if the baby had an air hole, he got one finger between the tiny, hard gums, which immediately closed on it and started sucking.

The soft cries were scarcely audible under the huge mound of stones. The father stood naked outside and rolled the stone back in front of the cave. He gathered smaller stones around it and finally put the spruce branches back in place. He listened again and walked a few steps in the direction he had come.

Then fear rushed in on him from all sides, fear for his child. It was safe from wolves, wild boars, and great horned owls, but he couldn't shut out the savage weasel, the cold snake, and the evil spirits. Holme returned to the entrance, examined it again, and shook a shivering fist out in the air at every terrible, dangerous creature wanting to eat the child. Then he ran through the forest moss, shot over the pine ridge, and flew from tuft to tuft through the white night mist in the hollow. The sedge slashed sharp and cold around his naked legs.

All the while he could feel the baby's gums close greedily around his finger, and he could visualize the mother's round, full breasts. He would unite them again; he ran faster and faster back the way he had come.

'Was that Ausi who went out?' a drowsy woman thrall asked a friend next to her.

'Yes, she probably can't sleep. Probably has some pain, too, from her milk.'

The thralls fell asleep again, but Ausi stood outside, wildly hoping to see Holme. Maybe he would come and tell her he'd found the baby. She had been watched herself until Stor and Tan had come back and night fell.

But out there, all was still. As she walked down the path toward the forest, there was a rustling in the refuse pile; a shadow glided out and moved off along the ground. Ausi could hear men snoring in the thralls' dwelling. Maybe Holme was inside sleeping, she thought bitterly. She had heard her friends say he was gone, but never before had a father gone out looking for his baby in the woods. Neither warrior nor thrall.

The forest was looming and black. Somewhere deep inside it her baby was lying on the bare ground, or maybe a wild animal had just discovered the little one and was closing its jaws around it. The thought doubled her over, forcing out a moan. As she walked up the path, the dogs growled in the warriors' hall, but a voice impatiently shut them up.

Where the woods grew more dense, she stopped and listened. A rivulet rippled softly down the slope, but there was something else, too. From the woods a panting noise was approaching; then something passed by her and stopped a little way below. She whimpered in fear before a naked body without head, hands or feet. The ghost leaned against a tree, breathed heavily and looked down over the settlement; soon she could distinguish its head and black shock of hair. Holme's sun-tanned face, hands, and feet blended into the darkness while the rest of his body glowed a soft white.

Her movement made him spin around, crouching in defense. She sensed more than saw his face relax when he recognized her, and in the midst of everything else she thought how strange he was, unlike any other man in the settlement. He was naked and he had probably been in a fight.

To Holme just then, the woman meant only food for the child lying under the stones. He took her arm and pulled her along with him as he uttered a few words to make her understand. But she already knew and ran beside the man she had hated and feared, happiness spreading through her whole being.

She felt the hot blood trickling down her legs from the fierce pace and as if in a dream saw the cool marsh where broad-winged birds flew toward them with anxious cries. She felt the warm gravel of the ridge under her feet and then the cool moss of the spruce forest again. While Holme rolled the stones away, she sat down trying to hide the blood that ran like black stripes down her legs. His white body ducked into a hole; she heard the baby squeal when it was touched, and then she had it in her arms.

The milk ran like a white thread down one breast while the baby nursed from the other. Holme stood leaning against a block of stone, looking on. He turned himself halfway away from the woman because he was naked. The threatening creases were gone from his face, and he looked calm and almost friendly in the first light of dawn. His garment lay beside the woman, and with one hand she ripped up some moss, wiped the baby's yellow excrement off the garment and handed it to its owner with an uncertain smile. She discovered with terror the blood on the child's leg, but the father said nothing about snatching it from the wild boar's jaws.

He had to go to the settlement again and knew it would be more dangerous now at dawn. But his ax and spear were still in the thralls' dwelling, his fishing tackle hanging next to them. The baby, full now, lay contentedly snorting at its mother's breast, but soon she would have to eat, too. Holme couldn't afford to be without his weapons and tools, not even one day.

Gently but firmly, he pushed mother and child into the cave, told her to stay there, and carefully covered up the entrance before he set off. Ausi readily obeyed, thankful the baby was alive. From inside the cave, she heard his feet running away. She wouldn't have thought he could run so fast; he always moved so slowly in the settlement, probably to annoy the chieftain.

The moss inside the cave was soft; smiling faintly, Ausi stretched herself out on it, as the child breathed lightly against her neck. A little way from her face there was a tiny opening between the jagged rocks, and gray light fell on a little patch of gravel and on a few pale blades of grass. After all the anguish, she felt endlessly calm and happy in the cavern, and she smiled again faintly in the darkness as she thought how long, long ago, people had actually lived in such places. She'd heard many stories about it.

Birds began chirping timidly outside. A pointed, black snout sniffed at the small opening; then its owner ran quickly off across the moss. The contours of the boulder slowly became visible in the cave, and Ausi could see that it reached inside a ways but that the rock ceiling got lower and lower.

As she fell asleep, she wondered where Holme had gone and how soon he'd be back. She hoped he wouldn't go back to the settlement, where he could be killed. But he knew what was best; she didn't have to worry.

A slight murmuring whispered in the treetops, and the uppermost layers of branches swayed. Then all grew quiet as the sun rose over the heathen land.

A couple of dogs got up out of the grass, yawned, and wagged their tails as Holme approached the settlement. He petted them and listened before he went into the thralls' dwelling. A couple of his friends drowsily stared up but didn't see anything unusual in Holme's being awake and so closed their eyes again.

He took his ax, his spear, his fishing tackle, and a few little things that belonged to him and went out again. As he walked outside toward the main building, he thought about the warriors and their bows. It would be good to have one. He also thought about the bread chest standing just inside the door.

He walked past a couple more dogs on the way down. They lay with their heads on their paws, looking up at him with brown, affectionate eyes while their tails swished in the grass.

The heavy door was not barred, and he carefully looked in. It was dark inside except under the hole in the roof,[1] where the dawn light fell through, spreading out on the floor below. He could see the fire pit's sooty oval opening and the warriors sleeping on the benches by the wall.

Silently Holme sneaked forward to the bread chest and opened it. It was filled with large, round disks of bread, and he threaded several of them onto his spear. Then he stood stock-still, his arms outstretched. A warrior had lifted his head and looked down toward the door.

Holme stood there a moment, expecting the warrior to raise the alarm. But the head sank down again and nothing happened. The warrior had probably been half asleep, not quite comprehending what he had seen.

The bows hung like an ordered row of half-moons, and Holme carefully lifted the closest one from its wooden peg. Everything was quiet as he went out again, closing the door behind him.

He stopped at the smithy. He couldn't be seen from there, so the danger was not very great. On one side of the forge lay large, rust-red clumps of ore and on the other side a row of ax-head ma-

1. Viking dwellings usually had a fire pit in the center of the floor with a smoke vent cut in the ceiling directly above it. On Viking architecture, see James Graham-Campbell and Dafydd Kidd, *The Vikings* (London: British Museum Publications, 1980), pp. 75–86.

terial. Holme took some iron arrowheads, a knife, a sledgehammer, and a pair of tongs with him. For a moment he looked at an almost-finished sword but shook his head and left it there. Swords were not for thralls; they got along best with axes and spears.[2]

Before walking farther into the woods, he looked out over the cove. A seabird was swimming beyond the belt of reeds, followed by a column of chicks, chirping eagerly. The surface of the water straight across and below the forest was calm and black. You could see the white ring in the water whenever a fish would jump, though it was very far away. The settlement was still quiet when Holme disappeared into the forest with his bread and iron.

The mist in the hollow was dissipating. You could hear various birds cry in an area overgrown with reeds and alderwood.

Holme laid everything down outside the cave, listened at the small opening, and sat down after he recognized Ausi's deep breathing, broken up by the child's quick panting. A boulder lay beside him with blueberry sprigs shooting up from a crack like bristles on a wild boar's back. He picked a handful of blueberries and ate them.

It gradually grew more and more light, until suddenly a tree trunk here and there shone a glaring yellow on its east side. In the distance among the trunks a glade lay in the clear sunlight. The air was cold and calm; the rocks had a translucent gray border around them, and their edges dissolved in light.

As he waited, Holme surveyed his treasures, one by one, with

2. Ebbe Schön, *Jan Fridegård och forntiden. En studie i diktverk och källor* (Uppsala, Sweden: Almqvist & Wiksell, 1973), p. 143, points out that Fridegård probably got the notion that different classes used different weapons during the Viking period from a museum catalog published by the University of Oslo in 1932: *Universitetets oldsaksamling. Tører utgitt ved samlingens bestyrer.*

pleasure. Then he hid them in the rocks, all but the ax. Fatigue crept over him, and he leaned back against the boulder. A little gray bird circled closer and closer, cocked its head, and peered at him. Finally it dared land and peck up the crumbs left from the bread.

One by one, the warriors awoke and walked out into the yard. Some went off to a pole nailed between two trees where they undid their clothes, squatted on the pole, and let their eyes wander across the glittering cove down below.

The thralls were already at work. Two of them let the pigs out of their pen and then followed the grubbing, grunting herd all day in the forest pasture. One swineherd carried a wooden container of meat and bread; a huge bronze horn hung over the other's shoulder. They always had it along, even though wolves seldom attacked during the summer. They appeared sometimes, fat and lazy, but drew away again with grinning jaws and wily eyes.

A few other thralls went off to the slope where they'd been breaking a new patch of land for some time. They had a small, long-haired horse and an iron-tipped wooden ard.[3] A couple had wooden spades with foot blocks and iron edges. Sweat ran down their grim faces as they labored in silence. Below them, they could see the warriors moving leisurely about the settlement or lying in the shade. Two were already reclining, one on either side of the game board,[4] contemplating it, their beards motionless.

3. An 'ard' is a simple pointed plow that cuts a groove in the soil but does not turn a furrow in it.

4. We have evidence that the Vikings played board games, although we do not always know exactly what the games were. One game, called *hnefatafl,* is a kind of chess that has only one king (the *hnefi*) defended by one group of games pieces (*töflur*) from another group. The game is mentioned in various places in Old Norse

18

Holme's two helpers sat by the smithy, looking indecisively down at the settlement. Their master was gone and they weren't used to doing anything on their own. They hoped to see him coming out of the woods before the chieftain woke up and came to the smithy.

The women thralls made their way to their own tasks. Two went into the high hall to straighten up after the night. Two others fetched grain from earthenware jars and carried it to the millstone. They spread the grain in the worn groove, crushing it into flour with a rock pestle. They swept the flour together with a bird's wing. You could hear a rhythmic sliding noise, and a little cloud of dust rose up into the sunlit air around the women at their milling.

While the women thralls worked, they talked softly about the two who had disappeared. Mothers had gone into the woods before, looking for their babies for days on end, but they had always come back and started working again. Their tears had dried sooner or later. But a father had never gone to any trouble before, as Holme had. Even so, they'd probably both be back soon, take their punishment, and everything would be back to normal.

The chieftain's wife hadn't slept well that night. She didn't think much about the baby abandoned in the woods, but she couldn't forget the look in the black-haired thrall's eyes, which augured revenge and misfortune. She feared no one else, but that silent thrall could do anything with his hands, coming as he probably did from across the sea where people had magic powers. She knew well enough that even the warriors took care not to mistreat

literature, *Hervararsaga* among them. See D. G. Calder, R. E. Bjork, P. K. Ford, and D. F. Melia, *Sources and Analogues of Old English Poetry II: The Major Germanic and Celtic Texts in Translation* (Cambridge: D. S. Brewer, 1983), p. 109, stanza 56.

him. As far as she knew, none of them had touched Ausi, but two of the other women had told her that they had seen Holme subdue her after a long fight. They laughed and said that in the end, she had thrown her arms around his neck to choke him.

From an angle inside the hall, the chieftain's wife saw the hole in the roof like a blue, bottomless well, and she knew that the sun had come up. She heard the pigs grunting, the birds singing, and a horse whinnying in the distance. The bearded chieftain lay by her side, and a smell of smoke and filth rose up from him. A ladybug entangled in his beard struggled for freedom.

A couple of warriors were snoring in unison out in the hall. Then the first fell silent, and shortly after, the second; a mosquito's shrill whine pierced the air. Blades of grass, small pieces of charcoal, and dry spruce twigs lay on the hard-packed dirt floor under her feet. A distant seagull's cry came down through the roof vent.

Her baby woke up and she pulled it to her breast, which was soon sucked dry. The child had light hair and large hands, and it kneaded its mother's breast while it nursed. She thought again about Ausi's baby and wished that the chieftain would allow some thrall children to live from now on. Otherwise, their own child would be without thralls when it grew up.

When the chieftain awoke and emerged from the hall, he didn't think about what had happened the night before. He walked past the flies swarming over the sunbaked mud of the pigsty, then beyond the slope toward the lake where he kneeled down and washed and snorted in the clear water between the rocks. Without drying his face, he took out a bone comb and started grooming his hair and beard. Now and then he bent forward to look at himself in the water and seemed pleased with his fat, coarse face and the wild forest of beard engulfing it.

When he returned to the settlement, the chieftain walked around to the different work areas. He didn't speak to the women thralls but gave stern orders to the men digging on the slope. They either gave no response or looked up malevolently beneath shaggy eyebrows. It was already blazing hot, and the little horse's matted coat glistened with sweat. After the chieftain had walked on, the thralls straightened up and silently watched the short, coarse figure. They were all tall and knew the chieftain didn't like anyone taller than he was.

As the chieftain approached the smithy, the two helpers started fiddling with tools so as not to look idle. One examined some long-nosed tongs and the other hammered a bent spearhead. They shook their heads when the chieftain asked about Holme. When he realized that the smith had run away, his furrowed brow turned redder than before, but he turned back to the settlement instead of saying anything to the thralls.

Very shortly, half the warriors armed themselves and went down to the shore. They hid behind the clump of trees where the memorial stones[5] stood, concealed by leaves at this time of year. When the leaves dropped in the fall, the stones became visible all the way up to the settlement, only to be hidden again with the coming of spring. The stones, standing on green mounds, had been raised above the chieftain's father and grandfather.

The warriors were set to attack the settlement. They took cover behind the trees as they advanced up the slope. When they were still at a distance, the clear, sharp twang of a bowstring rang out,

5. The memorial stones (*bautasten*) mentioned here do not have carvings or inscriptions on them. Those with carvings are called 'picture stones' (*bildsten*), and those with runic inscriptions or runic inscriptions and pictures are called 'rune stones' (*runsten*).

and an arrow sped like a white streak through the trees toward the attackers. It hit the ground short of reaching them, and the chieftain snarled angrily at the warrior who had shot prematurely.

From the clearing, the thralls snorted at such needless fighting. For them there was only the ax. That was good enough for both working and fighting.

The warriors had removed the iron tips from the arrows and had slackened their bowstrings. When the arrows started flashing back and forth between the two bands, they didn't come at deadly speed.

They shot at each other for a while, taking most of the arrows on their shields. One of the defenders suddenly leaped into the air to accomplish this, even though the arrow flew high over his head; you could hear the thralls mumble approvingly. The warriors fought silently; only the song of the bowstrings, counterpointed occasionally by clanging blows from the smithy, broke the silence.

At a shout from the chieftain, the warriors threw down their shields and bows, grabbed their swords, and charged each other. They hacked and parried a while, the broad iron blades flashing in the sun. The chieftain shouted again, the battle stopped, and all the warriors walked toward the settlement together.[6]

In a small cooking hut, two of the older women thralls were preparing the meal. They built a fire in the central fireplace and slid the meat onto the spit. When it was done, they carried it into the main building where the clay floor had been swept and cleaned.

6. According to Schön, *Fridegård och forntiden*, p. 144, Fridegård's description of Viking battle strategy was probably gleaned from the 1932 Norwegian museum catalog mentioned in note 2.

Two of the south window-holes were open, and sunlight streamed in over the rough table and benches. The dogs sniffed greedily in the doorway, but the women screamed menacingly at them to stay out.

The smell of the cooking meat drifted over the settlement, and those who noticed it turned toward the buildings. The thralls glared down bitterly; they knew that the worst meat was being cooked for them, even though they had been working since early that morning. An old woman was cooking it and when she was through, she fetched the driest, most poorly baked bread from the chieftain's wife.

After the old woman set the pot of meat on the table and put the bread beside it, she went out and called shrilly for the thralls. At the same time, she got a jar of water from the well.

The thralls ate in the half-dark inside. They clutched the meat and bread, panting like dogs. Occasionally one would pick up his ax and crush a bone with a resounding hack, then suck out the marrow. After the meal, the earthenware jar was handed around the table.

Work would not begin again until the worst heat had passed. The settlement rested silently on the scorched slope; no one could be seen for the next few hours. The dogs lay panting in the shade or gnawed on bones thrown out to them. Down below lay the cove; a budding field of flax, like a piece broken loose from it, was turning blue a short way up shore. A gull silently circled the settlement once before returning to the lake. Only the countless flies were constantly busy on the refuse pile and on the blazing hot timber wall above it.

When Holme woke up and took the stone away from the cave entrance, Ausi came creeping out, smiling. As Holme had done, she held the baby to her chest with one hand and steadied herself with the other. Both squinted into the strong sunlight pouring down over the hillside.

Holme held his ax so she would catch a glimpse of it, the corners of his mouth rising slightly with pride as she gasped in surprise. He showed her the other weapon, the work tools, and the bread lying there in a brown, delicious pile.

Ausi smiled again in happiness for the baby and the bread. A long time after waking, she had lain wondering what would happen to them. Hearing Holme's deep breathing outside, she had known that he hadn't left them, but how long would that last? One day he might be gone; he might get killed or just simply go his own way once he got tired of them. With his strong, skillful hands, he would be welcome wherever he wanted to settle down.

Holme turned back the garment to look at the baby. Scarcely a trace of the boar's bite was left. Holme's dark eyes smiled at the child's thighs, no thicker than his wrist. Ausi, who stood looking at them, realized that her eyes had never met his even though she had been closer to him than anyone else had. When he looked up, all you got was a feeling of piercing blackness. She saw those eyes clearing now, moving over the baby's body, anxiously searching, and she was glad.

Holding the child so the sun would shine on it, Ausi walked out onto the hillside. Below her the spruce thickets grew dense and mingled with the alder shrubs; there must be water there. Her feet sank into cool moss, and soon she came to a place where two glittering water veins met and gurgled gently out of a little hill coated with yellow-white lime. Ausi washed away the yellow excrement from the baby's body as it whimpered and struggled because of the cold water.

When the baby was clean, she peeked through the bushes toward the cave. Holme was nowhere to be seen; he must have crawled inside. With the child under one arm, she quickly loosened the brooches on her clothes, scooped up water with her free hand, and washed her body, which still bore traces of the night's strenuous flight from the settlement.

Afterward, in the shadow of the boulder, they ate their bread while the baby slept. They didn't say much; Holme was thinking about meat for the next meal, meat or fish. Ausi began thinking about how close the settlement was, and she looked around nervously. A roaming warrior could happen by; the swineherds might bring the pigs this way. They wouldn't hesitate to talk for some little reward or other.

Ausi wondered if Holme intended for them to stay here. He was in the greatest danger. They'd take her back, but they would surely kill him. And the baby would be handed over to Stor and Tan for the second time.

When Holme went out hunting, he took the stolen bow, his spear, and his knife with him. The sun hovered above the treetops and was already shining intensely on the east side of the cairn. From a nearby tree, a bird warbled endlessly, and the anxious, indistinct sounds of the lapwings rose from the hollow. On a mossy shelf made from two boulders, Ausi sat watching Holme walk farther and farther away until the tall, smooth-trunked pine trees on the gravel ridge blocked him from view. She saw with alarm that he was walking toward the settlement.

When Holme was about halfway there, he stopped and listened. He was more cautious now, looking carefully ahead. The marshy area extended for miles and created little lakes here and there, partly overgrown with vegetation. By the shore of one of these, the settlement's herd of pigs walked grunting and grubbing.

A few of them lay like gray blocks of stone in the cool mire.

Holme saw their herders a little farther away on a flat piece of rock. One was looking out over the marsh, but the other lay on his back with a huge water-lily leaf over his face to protect him from the sun. Beside the thralls, the bronze horn glistened brightly in the sunshine.

Holme thought for a moment about walking up to his companions and asking them about news from the settlement. Maybe they could give him one of the smaller pigs, too. One of them, Otrygg, probably would be on his side, but Krok would blab to the chieftain and the warriors. They would know he had stayed in the area and would search the whole district. Better to wait and not show himself; maybe the swineherds would fall asleep around midday.

Holme found a thicket where he could hide and look out over the little lake and herd of pigs on the shore. A school of small fish snapped at the air, making the water look like it was being pelted by a fine rain. Wild ducks and coots were quacking, and farther away a large brown bird hung flapping above the reeds. Two huge pigs started fighting, dancing, and squealing in the gurgling muck, ready to tear each other's bellies open. The thrall who was sitting up bellowed at them, looking around for something to throw.

The sun rose higher, and more pigs made for the mud. The thrall turned his head constantly in different directions, and Holme got more and more impatient in his hiding place.

Close to noon Holme caught sight of a swaying bush a long way from the herd. He kept his eye on it and finally saw the back of a medium-sized pig grubbing in the thicket.

Watching the swineherds, Holme crept the long way round toward the bush. He stopped nearby, expecting the pig to go even farther away from the others. But instead, it became uneasy, lifted its head, and listened. Holme had to act quickly.

He put the bow down, grabbed his spear, and crept a little to one side, putting the thickest bushes between him and the pig. When he was only a few feet away, he rushed forward, bursting through the thicket. The pig, its snout under a root it was trying to tear off, let out a terrified guttural sound and threw itself to one side but fell down, rolling over again on its back. In the same instant, Holme's spear went through its throat into the ground. The pig was nailed fast and, as Holme had expected, it had not had time for a single squeal.

Holme bore down on the spear, keeping clear of the pig's frantically pumping hind legs. Frothing, bright red blood gushed into the hole the pig's legs had just dug. Holme could hear two other pigs from the herd squealing as they fought.

Gradually the pig's writhing abated; Holme pulled out his spear and wiped it off in the moss. Then he walked until he could see the swineherds. Both were sitting on the rock now with the rucksack between them. Maybe they would nap after their meal. Most of the herd was in the marsh below the rock and would probably stay there until the worst heat had subsided.

Holme walked back to his motionless prey, its bristly white eyes shut tight in death. Big flies were already buzzing around the thicket. Holme had thought about covering the pig with juniper twigs and coming back for it at nightfall, but he changed his mind, deciding to take at least part of it with him. Ausi just couldn't wait until night for food.

Holme took his knife and cut around one of the shoulders to the bone. Then he stood on the other foreleg and yanked violently. The shoulder cracked and broke; he cut the sinews and pulled free a large, meaty chunk. It was easy to carry with the leg as a handle.

He covered the rest of the pig with fragrant twigs and then sneaked back. Both swineherds lay on their backs now. The pigs were rolling around indolently and scuffling playfully. Holme smiled maliciously at the thought of having deprived the chieftain of a pig. His black hair was heavy with sweat. Soon he was out of sight.

Toward evening when the thralls came home with the pigs, the chieftain stood as usual by the opening where the animals crawled into the pen, one by one. He held a long wooden staff, with a notch on it for each animal. He moved his finger notch by notch as the pigs crawled in, but one notch was left after all the pigs were inside.

The chieftain bellowed and yelled at the swineherds, who, tired and angry, had to trudge all the way back to the water-lily lake. They couldn't imagine that anything much had happened to the lost pig; maybe it got stuck in the mud. They didn't bother listening for it. They knew the pigs never squealed in the forest; they raised a terrible squealing and grunting only when the settlement was within sight and earshot.

Krok and Otrygg searched in vain for a long time and finally agreed that the animal must have gone out too far and drowned. The chieftain would stalk away from them, red in the face, but he wouldn't scold or beat them when it was clear that the pig was lost. They had known him for a long time, and he never made a fuss over something obviously hopeless.

All day Ausi wondered anxiously what the night would bring. Would Holme be with her in the cave? What would he do? How much did he understand, and could she talk to him?

Holme had gone to get the rest of the pig he had killed. They had cooked the meat on a flat rock with a fire underneath, but it didn't taste good without salt, and where could they get salt? The chieftain was very careful with his supply, which he got once a year in exchange for grain and iron from foreign traders. The meat wouldn't keep too long in the heat.

They had to think about moving on, too. The cave could be discovered any moment; every day the warriors wandered far from the settlement with their bows and spears. They might catch sight of the smoke and get curious. They knew where all the columns of smoke in the area should be, and if a new one appeared, everyone took notice and didn't give up until they knew where it came from.

They couldn't live in a cave indefinitely anyway. People had done that a long time ago, when they didn't know any better. Humans might even have lived in this very cave. Holme could build a house, of course, but they would have to go far away to be safe, deep in the countryside where farmsteads lay few and far between. And they'd have to do that before winter fell.

When Holme returned, he walked down to the spring with the pig's carcass and was gone for a long time. Toward evening, they ate a little meat and bread. The whole time Ausi thought about the moment they'd crawl into the cave for the night. She glanced at Holme from the side, but he never once turned his face toward her. What was he thinking about; how much did he understand?

Then he got up and started breaking twigs and carrying them into the cave. He wove a tight layer over the whole floor. Then he tore up big armfuls of the soft grass, warmed by the sun on the gravel ridge, and laid it on top of the twigs. Ausi should have put the baby down and helped, but Holme might think that meant he could sleep with her and the baby in the cave. It was best to leave him alone to do what he wanted.

But Ausi never knew whether Holme was planning to sleep with them or not. He was right behind her when she was ready to bend down and crawl in. She turned around anxiously, put her hand on his arm, and wouldn't let go until their eyes met. She was startled by the bitter passion in them but she didn't turn away. He knew immediately what she was thinking; she could see that and felt with relief she'd be safe. Now he could come in.

But he guided her gently in, showed her the best place to lie down, and then closed up the cave. She saw he had widened the opening between the stones to let more air and light in. The grass was soft and smelled sweet. She stretched herself out, smiling with satisfaction.

Holme could have slept in the cave, too, she thought before falling asleep, now that he knew she had to be left alone. But maybe he'd come in later. He probably still had things to do. She heard him now and then; he dislodged a stone and once he snorted like a dog. Then it got completely quiet, and you could hear the song-thrush even in the cave. But she sensed that Holme was very close by.

Holme sat on the rock with the blueberries on it, watching darkness approach through the trees. The sun shone now only in the tops of the tallest pine trees on the ridge. He heard weak, indistinct sounds, sometimes a distant call, sometimes a rustle or a thud nearby. He knew they came from forest creatures even though he couldn't see them. Maybe he could take them a token sacrifice, put a bit of meat and bread on a stone.

He could hear dogs barking in the distance; they stopped, then started again, and might easily be in the settlement. Barking carried a long way at night. He remembered they had to run out and pelt the dogs with rocks to keep them quiet when they started barking in the middle of the night for no good reason. But the older women thralls always shook their heads, mumbling about misfortune whenever the dogs started howling.

Now that things were quiet, he began thinking over all that had happened. He wondered what had come over him to run after a baby put out in the woods to die. Normally, no one ever did that, even if he knew he was the father. But Holme had had to do what he had done; his chest had ached strangely at the sight of the poor whimpering child at the chieftain's feet, receiving its scornful sentence. If he had been close enough with his ax or knife to the chieftain, there would have been trouble. But maybe they'd meet again.

A powerful snorting from the ridge caused Holme to crouch down and look up over the rock. After a while he could see something moving softly, something he had thought was a boulder. For a moment he saw the bear clearly silhouetted against the night sky; moving off, it hurried toward the woods on the other side of the hollow. Holme sat down calmly again. He had met the bear more than once before, and they seemed to agree tacitly to stay out of each other's way. But once he had seen an enraged bear — a spear and several arrows protruding from its body — almost demolish an entire farmstead.

When he felt his eyes growing heavy with sleep, Holme put the leftover grass down in front of the stone door as a bed. He kept hold of his ax. He heard the baby cry once, but the crying soon stopped, followed by a sucking noise. When it was as dark as it would get, he sensed something scurrying up to him. A small animal skittered across the rocks, its claws like rasps. But he felt cold when he got up, and so he sank back down among the rocks again.

The chieftain's child sat playing with some pinecones its mother had gathered. It reached out for more, and the mother picked them, murmuring and smiling. The warriors were busy with the boats by the shore; the thralls worked breaking the new field. It was cloudy, but warm and still, like just before a rain.

There was a thud next to the child, and a stone bounced in the grass. The child turned its head, looking at the stone with interest. The mother, sitting crouched down under a fir tree a little way away, didn't notice anything. She didn't see the second stone come whizzing either. It hit the child in the back just below the neck. She heard a noise and saw her baby lying still in the grass, its face ashen.

She snatched up the child and ran screaming toward the hall. The women thralls, terrified and curious, rushed forward; the men thralls straightened up and looked down the slope. They exchanged a few disdainful words, wondering what had gotten into the women this time.

From behind a boulder, a dark face looked out under a shock of black hair; then its owner slipped slowly from tree trunk to tree trunk until he was deep in the woods. There he picked up speed and was soon far away.

Holme, often drawn toward the settlement, had come upon a few things one night that could be of use to them in the cave: a bundle of cloth, a block of salt, a caldron with iron feet for the fire, a pair of scissors, and a few tools from the smithy. He wanted to see what people were doing during the day now since he was close by anyway. When Holme saw the chieftain's son in the grass, his hatred for the squat, scornful man welled up until he could hardly breathe. He would pay him back for a night not too long ago. The ground was full of good stones.

After running a while, Holme slowed to a walk. At first he was elated at hitting the chieftain's child but he soon began to feel uneasy. He knew that neither the chieftain himself nor any warrior would ever stoop to throwing a stone at or harming a child in any way. On the other hand, they weren't above dumping them in the woods to be eaten alive by mosquitos and ants or torn apart by wolves and foxes. He stopped while he thought about that. Maybe there was a difference somewhere, but he couldn't sort it out. He shook his head and walked on.

Holme knew what was happening in the settlement at that moment. A woman thrall would run down to the shore, screaming for the chieftain. He would come up the hillside, not running – that was beneath his dignity – but his short legs would move faster of their own accord. Once he had come up and gotten straight what had happened, it wouldn't be a good idea to be around. Holme smiled, thinking how everyone fled whenever the chieftain's face turned white instead of red, as it did for minor annoyances. Only one man stayed, the gigantic Stenulf. His job was to knock the weapons from the chieftain's hands, throw him to the ground, and hold him there until his face turned red again. Then the chieftain got up and was calm once more. Holme had seen it happen many times as he worked at the smithy. The chieftain would go inside without saying a word, and the warriors and thralls would emerge again from their scattered hiding places.[7]

When Holme got back, Ausi was sitting outside the cave. A soft, warm rain had begun to fall, and she soon crawled into the cave where the baby was sleeping. When Holme didn't come in after her, she stuck her hand out hesitantly and tugged on his clothes,

7. The chieftain's wild frenzies indicate that Fridegård probably means him to be a kind of berserk, perhaps even a caricature of a berserk, a warrior who derived his power in battle from Odin and was therefore invulnerable and not subject to the laws of society. For a discussion of berserks, see H. R. Ellis Davidson, *Gods and Myths of Northern Europe* (Harmondsworth: Penguin Books, 1964), pp. 66–69.

pointing to the place beside her. He came in but sat with his back to her, looking out through the opening.

'Did you go back there today?' asked Ausi, who missed talking with her friends.

'Yes.'

'What did you see?'

Gradually she pried out of him what had happened at the settlement. She felt intense, malicious glee thinking about the chieftain's child, but she was uneasy about the vengeance the chieftain would exact. He'd know what had happened. Then he would take all the warriors with him and scour the whole district. They'd better be on their way as soon as possible – as soon as the rain stopped. The cave was fine, but they had to live in a house like other people.

The rain increased, creating a gray stream outside the opening. Sometimes a breeze laden with a heavy smell of flowers and berries wafted into the cave. Through the hole between the boulders, big drops glided rapidly across the stone ledge and fell one by one on the gravel below.

It didn't stop raining all evening, and they stayed inside the cave. Ausi woke up once and through the hole saw a yellowish-blue sky; she knew the weather had cleared and night had fallen. Holme lay by the opening, sleeping noiselessly.

Ausi loosened the brooches at her shoulders and waist before she fell asleep again. A cool gust or two passed through the opening over Holme's body. If only she had something to cover him with, Ausi thought. But Holme probably wasn't cold – he was like iron and stone.

Everyone except the thralls clearing the new field gathered around the chieftain after his fit of rage had passed. He fingered

34

the blue welt on his child's neck, shaking his head silently at the mother's talk about trolls and other spirits. He looked around and found both stones.

'It was a thrall,' he said to the warriors standing around him, and they nodded silently. The chieftain looked toward the forest, estimating the distance from the large rocks lying among the trees farthest away. He knew now there would be no peace in the settlement as long as Holme was alive and free.

The child soon got a little color back in its face and started whimpering. An old woman thrall put an herb poultice on the wound, and after screaming loudly for a long time the child finally fell asleep. Within a few days, he had almost recovered, but the stone left a bump, and he couldn't turn his head. To look to one side, he had to turn his whole body.

After what had happened to the child, the chieftain set out guards at night. Holme, coming out to the edge of the woods to find a couple of traps, saw a tall figure outlined against the night sky north of the settlement. During the day, the warriors – two, three, or alone – roamed about in ever-widening circles from the settlement. Two of the dogs came up to Holme in the woods, licked his hands and wanted to follow him. He drove them away with the shaft of his spear, but they stopped a little ways off, looking longingly after him. One day they might lead the warriors to the cave, he thought.

It was probably best to move on. Other places, where he wasn't known, would be glad to have a smith like Holme. He had thought about just staying on his own, of course, but winter was coming, and living with a woman and a child in the cave wouldn't do.

Still there was no hurry. The nights were short and light yet, and a long string of warm days lay ahead. Then, too, Ausi needed to be a little stronger before they started a long journey. He had seen her wash off blood at the spring while she looked around apprehensively. They had to make clothes for the baby, too; it couldn't always be at its mother's breast. They had cloth, thread, and needles.

Ausi brightened when he told her some of his plans. She thought back on life at the settlement with greater and greater aversion now that she was away from it – away from the warriors who were too proud to look at the women thralls during the day but who came panting with lust at night, pressing them to the ground under heavy bodies; away from the thralls carrying repressed rage and treachery inside them; away from the quiet but dangerous chieftain; away from the gossip, the bickering, and the almost daily fighting among the women thralls. She was away from all that now.

The pork they had in the wellspring stayed good only a couple of days even though Holme kneaded it with the block of salt. It was tiresome, too, to have the same food day in and day out. The bread they had left was dry and moldy. There was plenty of fish in the small lakes, and Holme started putting his fishing gear in order. A hazel bush grew by the spring, and he cut himself a slender pole to tie the fishing line to. When he was ready, he told Ausi to take the baby and come with him, and she complied, happy and surprised. He was probably afraid that someone from the settlement might come to the cave while he was gone. But the danger was certainly just as great of someone running into them in the woods or spotting them by the lake. He had his weapons along, but what good would they do against two or more warriors?

On the way, she worried the baby would start crying, but Holme didn't think the sound would carry far because of the brush. Besides, the baby didn't cry often; it ate and slept, and for a while, it would squint into the light while it held on to one of its mother's fingers. Its leg had almost healed. Holme had looked at it a couple times with the hint of a smile on his bitter face.

When they reached the shore, Ausi sat down against a sun-warmed pine tree. Digging in the sand pile under the dead reeds that had washed up on land, Holme soon found a worm for his hook. Rushes and water-lily leaves covered almost all the water's surface, and he carefully lowered the hook between them.

He caught a fish almost immediately; it flopped down in front of Ausi after a glittering flight through the air. It had yellow scales and red fins. Holme, descending on it like a hawk, held it up in front of Ausi's nose while she laughed in delight. Holme flashed a smile too before starting to search among the reeds for another worm.

Farther out, a duck paddled out of the tall reeds, followed by a column of ducklings, but it turned around when it saw people. A pair of grebes fished a long way out, diving and shaking their heads when they surfaced. Dragonflies sailed back and forth over the reeds with a soft rustle of wings, past two others that were mating. Low yellow flowers grew in the short grass where Ausi was sitting, and a couple of bees, completely golden with pollen, wallowed in them. A brown bird with broad wings flew silently overhead, peering down on the humans.

The fish kept biting, and Holme soon had a glimmering pile of them in the shadow of a tree root. He threw the smallest ones back; they lay still a moment, belly up, before coming to life and vanishing. The hook caught on a lily leaf now and then and didn't come loose until the long, cylindrical stalk broke from its root to be yanked up with it.

Farther to the left, a little sandy point of land jutted out where the water was green and warm. The tiny, crystal-clear waters had cut ripples in the sand. Ausi walked there to wash the baby before they returned to the cave. The sand oozed between her toes, and the water formed cool rings around her legs as she waded out. Mussels had plowed small, serpentine trails everywhere.

She put the baby in the warmest part of the water, and its large head on its little neck hung heavily against her wrist while she washed it. The black hair on the front of its head rose and fell with the pulse.

Meanwhile, Holme strung a thin twig through the gills of the fish to make them easier to carry. By then it was afternoon; the shadows from the pine trees on the slope moved closer, and the water by the shore darkened. He untied the fishing line and hid the pole for another time. He took the hook and line with him.

When they reached the rise, they could see the woods on the other side of the lake. There was a glade in one spot, a square part of it shining a yellowish green, probably a field of grain. Gradually, they also made out a small gray building near the field. The hole in the roof was just a black dot. Two people at most could live there, maybe a couple of fugitives like themselves. Ausi felt a longing for house, home, and safety again, and even Holme walked pensively the rest of the way back.

After Ausi had settled the baby down on the fragrant grass bed, she walked to the spring to clean the fish. Holme, as usual, busied himself with his tools and weapons. As she walked past him, Ausi noticed his quick, bronze hands and the lock of black hair falling over his cheek. For the first time, she was proud he was hers. Little by little, her fear had disappeared, and she thought that it was his silence that had seemed dangerous to her before she had gotten to know him better. His foreign origin had probably disturbed her too.

In a cleft outside the cave, Holme had built a fireplace out of round stones from the ridge. After the fish were cleaned and washed, Ausi rubbed a fine dust off the salt block to cover them, and then she kneaded the salt in with her hands. She gathered dry grass to make a fire. Holme, looking in her direction now and then, took the tinderbox from his clothes and handed it to her.

Ausi had to strike several times before a tiny spark took hold in the grass and stayed alive. The spark would flicker and then catch on, helped by a soft breeze moving through the stones. The grass soon burned, and she stuck in a few dry white sticks before she put the frying pan on. When the pan got warm, she put in some of the pig's reddish-white lard, which had kept longer than the meat. Soon the fish were sizzling among the stones.

The smoke rose like a pillar, and Ausi looked up at it with concern. Anyone who stood on a rise might see it and realize that it didn't come from any settlement. It could lead the chieftain and the warriors there.

Ausi looked at Holme and saw her thought reflected in his face. He broke off a large spruce branch and came over to her. He fanned the smoke with the branch, forcing it to spread out along the ground. When it finally did rise, it couldn't be seen for long.

Once the fish were fried, Ausi put them on a rock next to her, then freshened the stale bread over the fire. Standing with tools in hand and working his jaws, Holme sniffed the air, but he didn't come until she called him.

Ausi heard Holme, busy just outside the cave, take a sharp, deep breath. She looked out, feeling terror paralyze her.

A warrior was standing a few steps from the cave – the gigantic Stenulf. He looked in surprise at the cave, the man in front of it, and the woman peering out. Then it all became clear to him and he nodded. Without taking his eyes off the warrior, Holme bent down and grabbed his ax.

Stenulf had his sword but not his bow or spear. He furrowed his brow at the motionless thrall and ordered him to follow along to the settlement. Ausi trembled, afraid he might obey but also afraid it might come to a fight. No warrior could defeat Stenulf. What could a thrall do?

The warrior didn't come any closer, and the thrall didn't move. The baby started making a fuss in the cave, and again Stenulf's face took on a startled expression. He must have come upon the cave by accident; he hadn't been out searching.

Again Stenulf ordered Holme to put down the ax and come along. His beard twitched in irritation, and he looked menacingly at his opponent. Ausi sensed that he'd prefer to be on his way but didn't think he could.

Even in the midst of the danger, she remembered that Stenulf had been the first one to pin her to the ground. She had managed to escape the warriors' and thralls' rough hands for a long time, but Stenulf's grip had rendered her powerless. She hadn't been able to do anything to defend herself. She thought he was going to do it again once, but it turned out to be Holme instead. Though she feared and hated Holme, she had been glad it was him instead of Stenulf.

When the warrior saw Holme wasn't going to obey, he hesitated. Stenulf didn't want to draw his sword on a thrall, but taking him bare-handed could be dangerous. Neither he nor any other warrior had ever given Holme a beating; he had gone wherever he wanted to, a silent warning emanating from him. In the smithy once, Stenulf had looked appreciatively at Holme's shoulders and arms as the sledgehammer danced, thinking they could handle anything.

A few steps behind Stenulf there was a big piece of wood that Holme had found and hauled back to make something of. Stenulf went for it, but at the same time Holme charged him with the ax, enraged by the contempt the warrior had displayed by not drawing his sword on a thrall. Stenulf parried the blow with the wood, but it was knocked flying out of his hand. He dodged quickly to one side so he could draw his sword before the next blow. Despite his size, he moved unbelievably smoothly. Now the thrall, armed with an ax, stood before the strongest warrior in the land, his broad sword drawn.

Ausi could see by Stenulf's face that he took his adversary seriously now. He stood with his knees bent slightly and kicked away a stone with one foot. Holme stood motionless again, waiting.

They stayed that way a while, but the warrior soon lost patience. He came at the thrall, who retreated, ducking the long sword as he tried to hack his opponent. Ausi expected at any moment to see Holme fall before the sword. She and the baby would be dragged back to the settlement, and the baby would be handed over to Stor and Tan for the second time. . . .

Ausi crept out and grabbed the spear leaning against the cave entrance. Holme had been moving in a half-circle, and Stenulf, following him, had his back to her. Ausi took the spear in both hands, rushed forward, and thrust it into Stenulf from behind.

A severe jolt almost knocked her off her feet, and the spear shattered in two. Stenulf had swung violently behind his back with his sword, catching the spear in the middle. As he did so, he lost balance, reeled, and was unable to parry Holme's blow fully. The ax grazed his neck.

Inexplicably, the fight stopped. Stenulf sheathed his sword and, with a look of arrogance at the thralls, walked up the ridge toward the settlement. Blood pulsed from his neck, and he hadn't gone far before it was flowing down one leg onto the ground. The spear had pierced the back of his clothes, but no blood showed. Holme and Ausi watched him until he reached the crest of the ridge, sank down the other side, and disappeared.

If he had condescended to turn around and look at his adversaries, his eyes, dulled by loss of blood, would have seen the man and the woman approach each other hesitantly, then rush together in an intense embrace. They reeled toward the cave, the woman crawling in first, her supple arms gripping eagerly after the man behind her. The baby cried for a long time before the mother drowsily clasped it to her chest, wet with milk squeezed from her breasts.

For a while they talked about not being able to stay in the cave much longer. They had to leave – not because Holme thought Stenulf would reveal how he'd gotten hurt; he'd let them think what they wanted at the settlement. They'd surely think he'd fought some warrior from another settlement. But their hiding place could be discovered again at any moment; soon Holme wouldn't dare leave mother and child alone while he was out getting food.

Holme didn't feel proud of the fight that had just taken place outside the cave. He knew well enough why Stenulf had walked away – because Ausi had jabbed him in the back. He knew it was beneath him to fight women and thralls. Holme thought he and the ax would have pulled through even without Ausi's help. He had kept clear of the long sword, waiting his chance to hurl the ax at his opponent's head and lunge for the spear at the same time. Then, if the ax hadn't hit home, the fight would have gone on.

Holme crawled out and looked at the traces of the battle. He had to make a spear shaft before they started their journey. He remembered with reluctant admiration Stenulf's swing behind his back. If Ausi had been standing just a little closer, she'd be dead.

He picked up the pieces of the shaft and put them with the others. Then he followed the trail of blood up toward the ridge. Ausi stuck her head out, watching him anxiously. Stenulf might not be too far away.

On the crest of the ridge loose boulders lay exposed, and Stenulf's blood painted a ragged ribbon across them. The sunny hollow lay far below with its tufts of sedge and cries of birds.

On the slope was a gigantic boulder, split in two. One part remained in place, but the other had slid down a few meters, plowing a deep furrow. In its shadow Holme saw something that made him stop, clutching his ax. There sat Stenulf, his head resting on his updrawn knees. He didn't move. His sword jutted out diagonally from his belt and seemed to prop him up.

Holme stood looking at him for a long time before moving closer. Stenulf had ripped a thick swath off his clothes and wrapped it around his neck. Seeing that, Holme knew his enemy was badly hurt, perhaps even dead. He moved closer, but Stenulf didn't move and didn't look up. His face was ashen above his beard and his eyes were shut. His whole left side was crimson with congealed blood. Holme went back to the ridge to find a place to bury him.

After Holme left, Ausi heard a bumblebee humming drowsily outside the cave. Now and then she caught a glimpse of it in the opening; there was moss underneath, and it probably had a hive there. Ausi had gone out after such hives many times and robbed them of their clear honey while the bumblebees buzzed around her hands or whined shrilly when they got stuck in the moss.

Why hadn't Holme returned yet? He'd been away a good while. Ausi got up to look for him and smiled at the tenderness in her shoulders where his powerful hands had recently clutched them.

The sun was setting, and the moss on the west side of the large rocks shone even brighter. The bumblebee still buzzed close to the opening. A little farther up she found some large, dark red, wild strawberries in a crevice, and she picked them for Holme.

She heard clattering and saw Holme standing waist deep in the ground. He had dug a large, rectangular pit. On one side lay a pile of stones and on the other, yellow gravel and pebbles he had scooped up with his hands.

In answer to her surprised question, he pointed silently down the slope. The sun had moved a long way since Stenulf had sat down in the boulder's shadow, and it shone on his bowed head now. His round cap had two straps crisscrossed over the crown. It took a moment for Ausi to realize he was dead, and then she thought there had been another fight. Neither had thought the neck wound could be fatal as they'd watched the massive warrior walk with dignified strides up the ridge.

It was, in any case, a great relief that Stenulf couldn't go back to the settlement anymore and give them away. They could stay there calmly now, at least overnight. Ausi gave Holme a couple words of praise before turning back to the baby, but he didn't answer or look up. The pile of stones grew, almost hiding him. The pit caved in constantly, making it needlessly large and irregular.

Stenulf was a heavy load to drag over the gravel and stones. His cap fell off and Holme retrieved it, breathing heavily from his exertion. Then he got down into the grave and let Stenulf slide over one edge while he kept clear of most of the blood. He arranged the warrior's body on the stones, undid the sword, and bent it double in toward his knees. Holme didn't know why he did that, but it was supposed to be that way. He vaguely recalled that the sword had to die too if it was going to be of any use to its owner on his journey.[8]

If they'd intended to stay in the cave, it wouldn't have been good having Stenulf so near. He hadn't been burned – no one knew what he might do. Only the burned could move; the unburned stayed where they lay. But how could Holme burn him alone? You needed a huge funeral pyre. The pyre would billow thick smoke for half a day, and many people would come to see what was going on. But this was unjust; Stenulf should have been burned and laid in a great burial mound.[9]

Holme shoved the finer gravel in first, but it didn't cover Stenulf; it ran down both sides and he was still visible. So he put a layer of round stones on top of him, but it wouldn't do to lay them on his face. Holme got out of the grave and walked down to the cairn by the cave. He had seen a convex piece of stone there that had broken loose from the side of a boulder and slid down into the moss. He would cover Stenulf's face with that.

After the second layer of round stones, only a few whiskers poked up between a couple of them. The third layer hid the tips of the toes, and then Stenulf could be seen no more.

Holme piled stones a couple of feet above the ground. Then he got a larger and heavier piece of rock from the cairn and put that on top. When he was through, he overturned the stones that Sten-

8. Schön, *Fridegård och forntiden*, p. 116, refers to the 1932 Norwegian museum catalog as the possible source for the notion of bending a dead man's sword before burying it with him. The catalog reports that bent swords have been found in Viking graves.

9. Although some scholars argue that the dead were frequently buried intact, others argue that in the area in which Holme lives, cremation was the rule. See Schön, *Fridegård och forntiden,* p. 115.

ulf's blood had dripped on so the red trail was less noticeable.

In the distance the sun was low, shining like clear fire among the trees. The gravel was warm under his feet, but the moss he stepped into was cool as water. Everything had gone well; he had overcome a powerful enemy, but he wasn't happy. He had no desire to crawl into the cave to the woman, even though he had just been thinking happily and with renewed yearning about doing just that.

Instead, he sat on a rock, letting his thoughts about leaving take more definite shape. In one way or another, people would soon know they were living in the cave; it could be surrounded at any moment. It would have been nice to stay where they were; finding a place among strangers would be hard. He'd get by, of course, but the woods and freedom would have been the best.

The chieftain wouldn't take Stenulf's departure so hard. He himself would be the strongest man in the settlement now.

Holme looked timorously at the mound where the warrior was pressed beneath many layers of rock. None of this was easy to understand. Just a little while ago, he had been standing there, wrinkling his forehead, huge and dangerous; now he was resting quietly under the rocks and would never rise again. Over there lay the pieces of the spear shaft he'd broken off.

'Holme,' Ausi called softly, but he didn't respond and she couldn't see him from the cave.

He had started thinking about what he should have done. He should have left Stenulf's body alone and sent a message to the settlement so they could burn him and put him in a proper burial mound. He and Ausi would surely have had time to escape. But he couldn't do it over again now; Stenulf would have to lie there unburned even though it wasn't right.

Holme's chest felt heavy from all the things he didn't understand. He looked at the trees, at the rocks, at his broad, coarse feet and shook his head. So much had happened the past few days, though he hadn't wanted any of it. He had been forced to do what he did.

In a little glade where the sun flooded in before setting, a meager swarm of big mosquitos played. The mound was bathed in the yellow evening light, and the long shadow of a pine tree divided it in two.

Holme's hands trembled and ached from scraping against the gravel, and he walked down and washed them in the spring. Ausi waited in the cave with cold meat and leathery bread. Her eyes took on a strange new expression when she saw Holme coming, shaking the water off his hands. He had given her a great and strange happiness that afternoon, and already she was looking forward to more. Then they would move on to a safe place and everything would be better. She felt completely recovered from childbirth, and her body was as clean and firm as before. They could move on the next day.

Holme closed up the cave more carefully than usual before they went to bed. He didn't look toward the ridge the last time he was out, but still he knew that Stenulf's mound stood out against the night sky. He thought with relief about how strong Stenulf was; maybe he could travel on even without being burned. He could probably throw the stones off. He ought to have meat and bread with him too, but what they had was nearly gone.

During the darkest time of night, a lean wolf, the fur scraped off its flanks, happened by. It caught the scent of blood, pressed its snout down in the moss, and snorted protractedly. Then it followed the trail to the mound and circled it a couple times. It stopped and wedged its muzzle between a couple of the stones while the fluffy fur on its back rose. A weak scent of smoke and human being coming from Stenulf made the wolf run in fear and rage down the steep slope toward the hollow where the night mist hovered above the coarse, cool sedge.

The wolf stopped by the shore, sniffing the area. A dog barking in the distance caused it to turn around and listen. Finally, with its tail swaying for balance, it stepped gingerly out onto the tufts of grass and made for the trees on the other side.

When Holme emerged, the forest was light and cool, but the sun wasn't up yet. In the dark cave, he had just seen the baby, still asleep, holding its mother's nipple tight in its gums.

Holme carefully closed the cave and put the dry spruce branch in front of it. But the ground there was getting trampled down – a path to the spring, like a line drawn through the moss and grass, was already visible and was even more conspicuous in the morning when the grass rose in the dew. It was time for them to leave.

He took his bow and a couple of arrows he had attached nail-sharp points to the day before. Beyond the spring was a large, dried-out marsh area where dwarf pine trees grew on six-foot high tufts of grass. Big, heavy birds usually perched there with blinking, fearful eyes and would rumble and flutter into flight when you were almost on top of them. He could probably sight one while it was still perched.

Tall, glistening grass hedged the area, and the soft blades brushing against his hand were damp. Cow trails wound through the tufts, which the cows liked to graze on. There were some fresh droppings, and a swarm of glittering flies was buzzing around them even though the morning was still chilly. Rotten tree trunks lay helter-skelter, twisted round with tendrils of grass. The area reeked of marsh tea and meadowsweet.

Holme walked cautiously, glancing from side to side, but a couple of heavy birds saw him first and took flight. He surprised a brown bird of prey eating a duck. It flew off, its victim still blinking though its chest was torn apart and half-eaten. The sun came up, shining through the thin needles of the dwarf pines.

Two small animals suddenly popped up in front of Holme and scurried off in different directions. They were light-gray rabbits, about half-grown. One sat down again after a few bounds, rose on its haunches, and looked around. Holme carefully put his bow down and searched the ground. He soon found a stick, a fresh branch from a dwarf pine, the twigs standing out on it like pins. The rabbit remained still, not running until Holme was right on top of it.

The chase was on, winding through tufts and thickets. Holme was just a couple of steps behind the rabbit when the ground turned to marsh and his feet sank. The rabbit got ahead but stopped when it no longer sensed the pursuer. The chase began again where the ground was firmer, and after a great effort, Holme managed to get close enough to hit the rabbit with the stick. It tumbled a couple of times, and before it could get to its feet again, Holme had thrown himself over it.

He went back to the bow, carrying the rabbit by the hind legs. It jerked violently, and Holme hit it with a rock to finish it off. It would be just enough to eat before their journey. They had plenty of cold, fried fish as provisions for the trip, and they could always get something on the way.

Ausi was still asleep when he returned, and he flayed the rabbit by the spring. A crow sat silently in the top of a spruce tree, waiting for him to finish and leave so it could take the entrails. He rinsed the small, reddish-blue carcass in the cold water and cut it in pieces before he pushed the stone away and woke up Ausi, who yawned happily at the new day.

When the meal was over, the fire out, and the skillet cool, Holme tied his belt around all their goods to make them easier to carry, leaving only the ax free. Ausi, who was shivering a little in the morning air, walked over into the sun on the east side of the cairn while she waited. She had tied her hair in a simple knot so it wouldn't swing loose during the journey. The baby lay in Ausi's arms, still looking up without expression into her face.

They had thought about following the ridge into the back country but had no more than skittishly passed Stenulf's mound when Holme stopped. He had gotten an idea, which he briefly explained to Ausi. They would go the other way, follow the shore along the cove to the settlement's mooring. When night fell, they would steal the rowboat. That would be much better than trudging through the woods in the daylight.

Ausi understood but was anxious about what might happen at the mooring. The chieftain had probably posted a guard by the boats when he realized Holme was around. Still, it would be nice to sit in a boat, skimming along the shore at night and hiding during the day. Who knew what they might run into in the woods?

Holme had already turned back, and once again they passed Stenulf's mound. Ausi cast a longing glance down at the cave – things had been good for them there despite everything. But soon the days would grow shorter and the nights colder; they had to have a house to live in like other people. A long time ago, people had lived in caves, but not anymore.

Holme walked barefoot in front of her; he needed a pair of shoes. She had her summer shoes on, but she would probably never again have her winter shoes with the fur still on the leather. She had left a few other things behind too: a necklace of wild-boar teeth and a white armband she'd gotten as a little girl from a warrior. Her friends doubtless had those things now and were glad she was gone.

They passed the spot where the pigs usually were, but not this early in the morning. A large area on the other side was black and chewed up. The lake was completely hidden under the water lilies and leaves.

It was just a couple hours' walk to the lakeshore, so they took their time. A few young spruce trees growing in a circle formed a small room with a shining green grass floor, and they stayed there half the day. It was quiet and warm; they could hear only the chirping of some tiny gray birds engrossed in plucking caterpillars from the spruce-tree trunks and the soft rustling song of the grasshoppers in the grass.

They each ate a couple of fish before moving on in the early afternoon. The closer they got to the shore, the larger the boulders on the ridge became, and the harder the walking got. Once they saw a little hut on the slope. Tall grass grew all the way to the smoke vent on its sod roof – there probably hadn't been a fire there for a long time. Holme went closer and saw that a whole stone wall had collapsed. The hut was worse than the cave they had just left.

Soon they heard the wind whistling softly in the treetops and felt the coolness from the lake on their cheeks. The ridge sank in a huge, even slope to the shore, and rocks glistened in the clear water as far as they could see. Even from the crest of the ridge, they could see small fish. There wasn't a boat in sight in the cove. Beyond the point of land, the waves were rolling and breaking, even though there was little wind.

Holme, in a good mood the whole day, talked several times about the boat and how much better off they would be with it. And they could really provoke the chieftain at the same time. Ausi agreed with him about taking the boat; Holme had worked the most on it and so it should be theirs. Just so everything turned out all right! Holme was too impatient to sit with her; he paced back and forth on shore, yearning for nightfall.

The baby fell asleep again, and Holme finally came and sat next to her. They talked quietly about the future and which way they should go first. They'd better keep hidden during the day and travel cautiously at night.

After a while, Holme took out his whetstone and started sharpening his ax even though it couldn't get any sharper. Ausi lay down and napped beside the baby. The sun neared the tops of the trees, the wind picked up a little, and small waves began to lap against the stones on the shore.

As dusk fell earlier, the dogs barked more frequently and for less reason than during the lightest summer nights. Holme stopped far from the settlement so they wouldn't catch his scent or hear his steps.

He saw no guard and heard no sign of life. The flax was still on the root, but the barley was harvested and laid out to dry. Holme would have liked to go to the smithy but didn't dare. Although the settlement was far away, he sensed its distinct odor, inhaling it with a curious longing in his chest – the smell of soot, bread, and the garbage pile.

Holme walked down to the shore, emerging a short distance from the settlement. He noticed at once that the long ship was gone and felt great apprehension before he got close enough to catch sight of the little rowboat. He listened again before approaching it but couldn't hear a sound from land or lake. The warriors were probably either out on a long journey or waiting by the small islands to ambush some merchant ship.

He untied the boat, and it grated slightly on the stones as he pushed it out. No one yelled or threw a spear or shot an arrow at him. He rowed silently along the reeds, occasionally hearing a terrified quacking and splashing in them.

A cow suddenly bellowed among the alder bushes, and Holme stopped rowing in alarm. He heard a few snorts and the sound of twigs breaking. Ausi stood close to shore, trembling with anxiety and cold as Holme emerged from the reeds that thinned out and ended by the rocks. When he approached shore, she was glad to see a couple of old skin rugs lying in the prow. She had seen them before, and she knew that the warriors used them in bad weather when they were out fishing in the cove.

Through the darkness, Ausi saw Holme's teeth gleaming triumphantly. He didn't say anything about the warriors being out in the long ship; he didn't want her looking around. He could both row and keep a lookout himself and she could rest.

Holme rowed silently. The darkness grew more and more dense, then lightened again over the lake and land. Ausi dozed in the stern with one of the skins over her, awakening only to see if her baby was all right. Sometimes the reeds opened up, and Holme could sense a farmstead by the faint smell of smoke, a horse neighing, or a boat lying on the shore. At dawn, it got cooler, and light mists floated across the water. The islets farthest out seemed like black streaks and dots against the sky, rising red from the lake.

For a while after the chieftain's child had been hit by the stone, the warriors roamed around, hunting the fugitives. They weren't very happy about it either, preferring to believe that Holme hadn't dared stay around after what he had done. Hitting the chieftain's child was probably just his parting gesture.

The thralls lived in suspense from morning to night. They

looked toward the woods constantly, unable to rest until the last warrior had come back at night empty-handed. Then they were content; it was like a victory for them. They predicted misfortune for the warrior who ran into Holme alone, and his helpers at the smithy were sure that even two warriors couldn't bring him back against his will.

The women's suspense was even greater. They never tired of guessing what might be happening to Ausi. Unlike the men, most of the women would have been happy to see her brought back and punished. Their disappointment was clear every time the hunters came home without their quarry. The chieftain was silent, but his face was red and the furrows in his brow deep. Stor and Tan ran around officiously on the little patches of field, pushing their companions about when the chieftain approached. Everyone except Stenulf felt uneasy when he was around.

The boy had almost recovered, but he still had to turn his whole body to look to either side. The mother never let him out of her sight again, and she looked mistrustfully at the woods whenever she was outside with him. The chieftain had finally convinced her who had thrown the stone, and it wasn't a troll.

While the grain was drying, the settlement's inhabitants were busy harvesting leaves. It was over an hour's journey to a deciduous area where the surrounding farmsteads each had a designated place to harvest. People swarmed everywhere with knives, hacking and chopping. Small, shaggy horses hauled the fragrant harvest away on low wagons with oak trundles for wheels. Those without horse and wagon carried the harvest, bound with leather thongs in big bundles, on their backs. People were everywhere on the slopes and meadows where there was grass, cutting it off to dry, but without the harvest there wouldn't be enough winter fodder. As it was, the cows, sheep, and goats stayed outside as long as they could feed themselves. Their coats were thick from the cold, and they tore heather and moss up from the snow with hardened muzzles. During the long, cold nights they roamed the farmsteads crying out loudly, drops of ice hanging like glittering wreaths from their mouths. Only the hairless pigs had to be kept inside, and they would answer the snorts of their freezing companions from their sod-covered sty, a rectangular mound beneath the snow.

When Stenulf didn't come back, there was great wonder in the settlement. He couldn't have gone back to his old farmstead; it was many days' journey away and he was feuding with his father and brothers. And he couldn't have joined another chieftain, because his weapons and other belongings were still there. Something must have happened to him. No one imagined that a single man could have killed him. Who could defeat Stenulf?

The warriors started searching again as soon as they could. The hay and leaf harvest demanded every man's attention, and there wasn't much spare time. A warrior following the ridge happened upon Stenulf's mound. He noticed that it was fresh but didn't see the cave or the traces of blood. He didn't think either that there was anything especially peculiar about the thousands of flies buzzing around the mound or sitting motionlessly on the stones, almost seeming to think. The warrior shook his head, more bearded than wise, and walked on. He failed to notice the faint smell of corpse on the lee side of the mound.

Stenulf's bench remained vacant with the black and yellow shield and his bow above it. A few warriors mumbled about black magic; some thought he'd run into a wounded bear. Only the chieftain suspected Holme. He knew that the dark, silent thrall was dangerous enough with an ax or a spear in his hand.

After most of the harvest had been brought in, the warriors stopped working, leaving the rest of the job to the thralls. There was still the flax to cut and lay out to rot; the clearing wasn't finished yet but the thrall foremen, Stor and Tan, were to see to it that everything was done. The warriors started making the long ship ready for a fishing voyage. The big fishbasket by the shore would soon be empty.

The ship had six pairs of oars but no dragon's head on the high prow. The sail was yellow and black. When the wind was up and the oars drawn in, the warriors sat with their shields over the side, alternating the black and yellow. It angered them that the ship wasn't larger and didn't have a dragon's head, but the chieftain often talked about calling in a shipbuilder to build a bigger ship. There was a clump of tall, young oak trees near the shore that he eyed frequently.

The second day out, they saw something approaching from the north: three dragon ships with furled red- and white-striped sails and rows of shields of the same color. The warriors rowed behind an islet, stepped ashore, and watched the foreign dragons approaching at a good clip. They passed very near, white foam rising before the gilded prows. The dragon heads – huge red mouths gaping among the gold – gazed relentlessly toward a distant adventure. Fourteen warriors sat on each side of the ships, their round helmet caps visible over their shields. One man sat in the stem of each ship and another in the stern by the rudder. They soon passed, and the warriors saw the dragons' wakes, which were sucked hissing along after them.

Great dissatisfaction took hold of the men by the islet. They looked contemptuously at their own ship and almost threateningly at their chieftain. A furious longing to sail out, far out toward the west, gripped them at the sight of the departing dragons. They walked around the settlement summer and winter just like thralls, and it was never any different. It would be better to join a chieftain like the one who had just sailed by.

Even their chieftain looked at the dragons with disappointment and envy, and he renewed his promise to build a ship. They would fell the oaks that year so the construction could start the following spring. But the warriors remained sullen and troubled during the whole fishing trip.

When they approached the mooring, Tan and Stor were standing at a distance, frightened, calling out that the little boat had been stolen. Who could contain the chieftain's rage now that Stenulf was gone? Something bad would surely happen. They called out in unison that Holme had probably stolen the boat, then moved up the slope out of danger.

The chieftain, angry already, turned white and hard in the face. He ground his teeth furiously, but the warriors stayed there in a grim group. They were angry too and felt no desire to get out of the chieftain's way. A spark of reason still flickered behind his wrinkled brow, but his rage had to have release. He slung his arms around a huge rock, carried it over, and threw it into the water with a violent splash. The color returned to his face, and he walked quietly up the hill. From the settlement, his wife, her child on her arm, looked apprehensively at him, and the thralls stood erect in the field. But the chieftain just calmly asked which night the boat had disappeared. When he found it had been two days before, he gave up all thought of pursuit. They would just have to make do for the rest of the summer with the big boat. When the boat building began, they could use the leftover timber to build a new boat for traveling among the islands.

Gradually the chieftain began to be glad that Holme had left with the boat. He knew that the dangerous thrall wasn't nearby.

The chieftain no longer had to fear for his wife and child when he was away. His biggest problem now was finding a smith as skillful as the one he had lost.

When the sun reached its peak on the second day, Holme and Ausi saw a vessel in the distance. It looked odd and could hardly move in the warm wind. Holme rowed the boat into the reeds and forced it close enough to shore so they could wade to land and escape if they had to.

They couldn't see anything through the tall reeds, so Holme waded to shore and watched the slowly approaching vessel. He sat on a bare hill, grunting an occasional word or two in answer to Ausi's anxious questions. Behind him rose a dense pine forest, carpeted with thick, green moss.

Holme was soon convinced the vessel was a merchant ship and posed no threat. He was just about to wade back to the boat and move on when he caught sight of something else behind the wooded point to his right. A dragon ship appeared in the sparse reeds; the head seemed to rise above the reeds to gaze out. Behind it came a second, then a third. They had been hiding behind the point. The foreign vessel was almost even with them, and Holme could see men running frantically around on it.

Holme called softly to Ausi, and she immediately came wading ashore with updrawn skirt. The baby was asleep in the boat a few steps away. The dragons picked up speed, their heads gleaming brilliantly in the sunlight. Then they burst out of the reeds, and fourteen pairs of oars apiece propelled them toward the foreign ship. The men on it lined up by the rail, long swords glistening in their hands.

Two warriors on the closest dragon slammed their axes into the ship and held on. The two other dragons hauled to on the outside of the first, and the warriors on all three rushed on board the vessel. There was a short fight; a couple of the foreigners fell, and some were shoved overboard. Holme and Ausi could hear them splashing. The men sank immediately and did not rise again. The others soon capitulated and were disarmed.

Holme and Ausi could make out an unarmed figure clad in a long garment, holding up something shiny. The warriors encircled the figure as if they were listening to its words. It couldn't be a woman because he was as tall as the biggest warrior and had broad shoulders.

After a moment's deliberation, the warriors' chieftain motioned for the strange figure to get into the closest dragon ship. He obeyed after lifting his hands above the prisoners – his companions – that he was leaving behind. The warriors rowed into a cove, disappearing behind a point of land. Holme and Ausi stayed hidden, watching those on the lake who were getting ready to take the foreign ship in tow. The disarmed men had to stay on board.

The third dragon returned without the foreigner, and when everything was ready, they rowed toward the north with their booty in tow. A belt of reeds gradually blocked the ships from view; only the dragons' gilded necks could be seen for a moment more over the brown spikes.

Once the dragons were gone, Holme pushed the boat out of the reeds with a pole, staying close to them as he rowed slowly. Behind the point of land was the cove where the warriors had lain in wait and where they had put the foreigner ashore. There was a narrow sandy shore, and the clear water looked black against the woods behind it. The thralls, peering cautiously ahead, could see the foreigner still there on shore. He was leaning forward on a stone, holding his face in his hands. Anybody could have sneaked up on him from the woods and killed him. You could tell that he came from far away, Holme thought, looking at him in wonder.

After a moment he took his hands from his face and rose to his full height. They could see his face from the boat now, a light, beautiful, and beardless face, unlike any they had seen before. Ausi whispered to Holme to row away; he was probably a sorcerer with the power to destroy them. He took out the shiny object, raised it toward the sky, and called out some strange words that made the thralls shiver.

Holme knew then why the warriors had put the foreigner ashore. He was a sorcerer; they didn't dare kill him or take him with them. He was probably busy even now calling down a storm or some other evil on the departing warriors.

The foreigner put the shiny object away and started walking toward the woods without having seen either the boat or the two terrified faces staring out among the reeds. He walked calmly, not looking around even though he had no weapon. Holme surmised that he didn't need to fear arrow, spear, or ax. Soon the tall, gray figure vanished among the trees. Toward the north, they could still barely make out the dragons and the booty, just a row of dark specks.

Holme rowed to where the foreigners had fallen into the water, but there was no trace of them. A tinge of red in the water indicated they had been cut down by swords and tumbled overboard.

Toward evening of the second day, they ran into a mild current. Holme tasted the water, and found it less salty there.[10] Several

10. Fridegård apparently intends for the settlement that Holme and Ausi are fleeing from to be in east Sweden, near the Baltic Sea. As they row west on Lake Mälar toward the Viking market town, they move into fresh water.

times they had to get out of the way of ships coming up on them or bearing down. But the people on board paid no attention to the fugitives who were keeping as close to shore as possible.

The shores and islets had grown steeper and rockier; they no longer saw many farmsteads or animals. The thralls slept a couple of hours in the boat, then continued at first light. They saw several boats by the shore, but their occupants – except for one, who kept watch – were asleep under skin rugs on the beach.

The countercurrent got stronger and stronger until they reached the spot where it came rushing down on both sides of an island. They rowed against the western current, but had to step ashore where it was strongest. Holme waded along, hauling the boat behind him. Fresh water was above the current, and a ways beyond the round islet was a long island where they saw people harvesting leaves on the slope by the lake. In front of them on both sides stood dark, towering fir forests.

The farmsteads were closer together here than they had been below the current. They saw grass-covered roofs and small white cows everywhere. Farther back, the land sank down again and there was plenty of deciduous forest. Holme and Ausi looked apprehensively at all the buildings and longed for their cave.

Toward afternoon, they saw a little, solitary hut in a sparse fir forest a short distance from shore. They decided to land and ask around. A dense belt of reeds by the beach provided good cover for the boat.

It felt good to have solid ground underfoot again. Before them lay a meadow filled with tussocks. Farther away, it rose in wavelike plateaus, densely covered with prickly green thickets and several varieties of small trees. No one was in sight, but numerous animal trails wound here and there, crisscrossing through the brush.

The sparse fir forest began behind the scrub brush. The little hut was made of mud and stone; from a distance, they saw a man sitting on a bench outside it. When he saw them coming, he got up and went into the hut, coming out again immediately and leaning the ax he had fetched beside him against the bench.

Ausi stopped short with the baby, and Holme went on alone. The man looked at him calmly, cordially answering his questions. The market town was a half-day's journey away, and they could get everything they needed there.[11] He also thought that a skillful smith would be well received wherever he wanted to settle down. If they wanted to stay with him for a night or more, there was nothing stopping them.

The man got up and opened the door. He left the ax behind by the bench; seeing that, Holme did the same. Ausi came closer and the stranger invited them into the dusky hut. There was a table, a few benches, and a round fire pit inside. The ceiling and walls were covered with narrow square timbers, but the mud stuck through a little everywhere and had plopped down here and there onto the floor, the table, or the benches. A tripod, a frying pan, and two caldrons stood by the fire. White, crafted wood – a bucket, tankards, bowls, and spoons – glowed in a corner. Holme inspected them more closely and nodded approval at the craftsmanship. Their host took out bread, cold meat, and water.

They didn't talk about themselves, but Ausi thought the man had been a thrall just like them. After they had eaten, he said he usually rowed to the market town to sell his wooden wares once he had enough of them. He said something about their probably meeting again if they, too, were planning on going there.

11. Fridegård never mentions the name of the market town, but it is unmistakably Birka, a major Viking trading center that was established around A.D. 800 and flourished for about two hundred years. Its ruins lie about twenty miles west of present-day Stockholm.

In the evening he took out a couple of skin rugs for his guests and let them have the best benches. He went outside to get the door, which had no hinges but did have a heavy iron ring and a wooden bar. It would be impossible to get in without tearing the hut down. Holme wondered why the man had such a sturdy door.

The wind had started up, and a big spruce tree on the east side swayed back and forth above the hole in the roof, spreading light and shadow on the floor beneath. A whistling wind rose and fell. The hut's owner lay awake for a long time, burning with desire for the woman, but whenever he moved, he sensed the man's watchfulness permeating the room. He had also perceived that he would come out on the short end in a fight with the dark thrall. The woman and baby slept calmly as the sound of the wind descended through the opening in the ceiling.

After the stranger from the plundered ship had been put ashore by the Norsemen and had seen them disappear with his vessel and its survivors, he walked aimlessly into the woods. He had seen respect and a reluctant timidity in the pirates' eyes, and in that he saw God's hand. He didn't know they thought he was a sorcerer. They didn't dare rob him of his gold cross, which he had held out as a shield. Many of them wore metal objects around their own necks, shielding them from misfortunes of many kinds.[12] They considered him strange and wanted to be rid of him.

He no longer thought about his men who had been killed in the fight. He had seen much and knew that wherever his faith had gone forth, it had left bloody footprints behind.

12. Worshipers of Thor often wore amulets in the shape of Thor's hammer, Mjöllnir, which Thor used to protect himself and the other Norse gods. The amulet resembles a crucifix.

When darkness fell, he still hadn't seen a person or a dwelling place in the strange, heathen land. He ate a few berries, drank water from a brook, and lay down to sleep where the rising sun would shine on him. He didn't know what kind of dangerous animals lived in the northern land but was sure they wouldn't touch him. That the wild pirates hadn't killed him he took as a sign that he'd accomplish his mission.

He woke up once in the gray morning light and saw an animal, a dog, sniffing at him from a few feet away. When the animal met his eyes, it snarled, but slinked off, its hackles up. When it was a little ways away, it fell into a lopsided trot, one eye glancing nervously behind it. The stranger laughed, turned over shivering in the moss, and waited for the sun to come up. He saw the insects, which the evening before had sunned themselves on the west side of the rocks, come crawling over to the east side to wait for the sun, just as he did.

He suddenly thought he heard the weak clang of a bell and realized he had heard it a moment before in his sleep – a muffled, beautiful sound that came closer and then died away. Could it be a heavenly bell encouraging him, telling him he was on the right path and need only proceed? In this heathen land, deep in the wilderness, there couldn't be any real bells.

He heard it growing distant, going away, and he felt himself strengthened and full of power. And the small cows, one with a bronze bell around its neck, walked onto their farmstead for the morning milking.

The stranger ate red berries growing around the stones on the slope before going on. When the sun reached its peak, he was able to get some bread and fried fish from a couple of staring, terrified women by the shore, and was reminded that his Lord had once blessed such food. He tried to talk with the women, but they gathered up their things and left. They were carrying plaited baskets full of some kind of root they had dug up with straight knives.

From a high hill, he could see the lake winding into the distance. Large and small ships went in both directions, some with gilded dragon heads like those that had captured his vessel. Finally, he recognized a broad, Frisian vessel approaching among the islets, and he smiled victoriously. He was on the right path and merely had to follow the shore.

Farther inland, the land sank and the forest became more and more mixed with deciduous trees. Passing the heathen farmsteads, the stranger saw people busy with their patches of land or carrying leaves in big bundles on their backs. Everywhere, dogs rushed out at him, barking, and the heathens kept a watchful eye.

The stranger saw many people gathered around a large, dirt-black mound in a clump of birch trees, and there was the smell of a fire. Before he could get any closer, they had all gone off toward a distant farmstead. The stranger saw a stone they had dragged up, probably to stand on the mound, and beside it lay a big, still-smoldering pyre. The heathens had dug up the earth around it for the mound, leaving a few of their spades behind. Beyond the new mound, you could see others the same size, green with grass and topped with stones.

Here, too, the dogs rushed at him, barking wildly. Some men came out and looked down toward the grove. The stranger kept going, but the dogs didn't quiet down until he was far into the woods.

When night fell, he was still wandering on, trying to keep the shore in sight. The land had become more desolate again, filled with wild thickets or dark, mossy forest. In the darkness, he walked past a little hut made of peat moss and stones. It smelled of smoke, but a stout wooden door sat in front of it. The wind had come up; the tops of the spruce trees swayed and whipped back and forth high in the sky above the low earthen hut. Between gusts of wind, he could hear the never-ending barking of dogs that they had been able to hear from the ship and that had followed him through the woods, near or far.

The day had dawned a little by the time the stranger came down to the shore again. A low boulder went in steplike progressions down to the water, and he found a calm and protected place. Above him, the wind took hold of the branches and angrily shook them. Far away on the lake, he could hear shouting, but he decided to wait for daylight to try to see across. His journey's goal was on an island; maybe he'd be there soon. He who subdued the storm, the wild animals, and the heathens was with him guiding his steps – he couldn't get lost.

He fell asleep and heard the powerful wind even as he slept. But the storm subsided with the warmth of the sun, and it was almost calm when he woke up. He went down to the shore and looked around. To his left was a sandy point of land with footprints on it and signs that boats had been drawn up. He decided to wait there until some boat passed by or perhaps some person on land.

The lone man in the dirt hut followed his guests to the boat and showed them which way to row. It wasn't far; they could be there before evening. He went out in the water and helped Holme get the boat loose from the dense reeds. From the lake, they watched him walk into the grayish-green waves of brushwood and disappear.

Farther out, there were still whitecaps on the lake. A long vessel with many pairs of oars fought against the waves, winning slowly. Another ship, its sails furled before the wind, approached from a distance at a sizzling speed.

Holme and Ausi kept offshore the whole morning. The man in the hut had told them about the town, and Ausi was curious to see it. Holme sat silent and would rather have rowed in the other direction where there were large, unpopulated areas. The many strange-looking vessels made him uneasy.

In one place, where the reeds were shorter and sparser, a sandy point of land protruded below a boulder. Holme rowed toward the point so they could land and rest a while. There might be plenty of fish by the point, too.

Both Holme and Ausi had walked up onto the shore before they caught sight of the stranger. He was sitting on a rock again, and they recognized him immediately. They didn't know that the distance he had walked wasn't half what they had rowed, and they stopped in astonishment. Holme clutched his ax, but the man stood up and walked toward them with a friendly smile. He carried no weapons and probably didn't need any. The object they had seen him raise in the air hung on his chest now.

Ausi retreated behind Holme, apprehensively hiding the baby from the stranger's eyes. She heard his voice but didn't understand a word. He pointed across the water in the direction the ships were going, then at himself, then at their boat. She hoped Holme wouldn't take him along, although it might be just as risky not to.

Holme soon decided he didn't need to fear the stranger. He had heard the warriors talking about merchants from distant lands who talked strangely; this man was probably one of them.

The warriors who put him ashore had probably been afraid he was a sorcerer or posed some other threat. Or perhaps they knew him and didn't want to do him any harm.

Among the foreigner's words, Holme heard the name of the market town, and he thought it probably wasn't too far away. He whispered to Ausi to sit in the bow with the baby and let the stranger have the stern. Then he could keep an eye on him while he rowed.

Behind the next point of land, the lake spread out almost endlessly in front of them. Two or three boats within sight went diagonally across to an island with a couple of larger islands beyond it. Holme rowed toward them, and the stranger nodded. He looked with kindness at the thralls, and Ausi thought that if they did him a service, maybe he could do something for them in return. He looked noble even though his clothes were simple. His hands were clean and white, and she could see a band of fine cloth around his neck under the gray cape.

The baby began to get restless at her breast, and Ausi tried to turn so it could nurse without her having to expose herself. She finally managed after a lot of trouble and looked apprehensively at the stranger. He sat looking around. The soft smacking noises the baby made while eating were obscured by the sound of the waves lapping against the boat. Ausi met his clear gaze a couple of times but turned quickly away. His eyes radiated a cool friendliness she had never seen before. The warriors were sullenly proud and vain, but this was different. Ausi felt that people like her and Holme should obey and serve a man like the stranger. He was above everybody and probably wouldn't even fear Stenulf, if the warrior were still alive.

At a distance they could see a number of vessels anchored off a point. Some distance up on the land, a gray stone tower jutted out of the leafy forest. The market town came into view, but Holme and Ausi still didn't comprehend that what they saw on the shore around the tower were numerous buildings.

When the stranger saw the market town, he said a few words and looked toward the sky. Holme rested suspiciously on his oars, glancing stealthily at his ax. He probably shouldn't trust the stranger more than he had to, although fortune did seem to be with him – the wind kept dying down more and more until there were no whitecaps to be seen.

Holme looked at the town a long while, then set course to a peaceful and unpopulated-looking place well to one side. The stranger nodded again, seeming to be of the same opinion.

They saw people, many with large burdens, moving in a constant stream between the buildings and the shore. Some men on horseback came across the flatland from the west. Around the whole enclosure was a high palisade with intermittent towers, probably by the gates.

The shore wasn't really unpopulated anywhere, but they landed at the calmest spot – a few children playing, a couple of small patches of tilled soil, and beyond them, a small hut. A little fishing boat had been pulled up into the sand.

Once ashore, the stranger nodded a friendly farewell and walked directly to town. Ausi watched him with relief mingled with disappointment. He must be a powerful man and could have helped them somehow. She said so to Holme, but he grumbled indifferently as he dragged the boat far up on the beach.

Holme bundled up the skin rugs to take along; they would come in handy if they had to sleep outside one night or even longer. He wasn't sure they would stay in town. He would rather have rowed on toward the great, dark-forested landscape on the horizon.

A broad, well-traveled road cut through two stands of scattered trees. They met many people on it, but no one paid any attention to them. Ausi was surprised to see a woman dressed in gold cloth with several women thralls trailing behind her. She must be some great and wealthy chieftain's wife or perhaps the queen herself. She looked at no one, sticking her nose in the air as she walked ahead, glittering. Holme looked furtively at the train but didn't respond to Ausi's admiring chatter and speculations.

Apprehensive about the reception they might get, Holme decided to leave Ausi and the baby some distance away while he walked in alone. If he was attacked, he could fight or run, but what could they do?

When they were near enough to see the people hurrying between the boats and the buildings, he told Ausi to stay where she was and wait for him. He left everything with her except the knife, which he kept concealed in his clothes.

Ausi sat on the skins, uneasily watching Holme go. He talked with a man who came out of a gate, and she expected to see them start fighting at any moment. The man was fully armed with sword and shield. He pointed toward the gate, and Holme went inside but came out again immediately and returned quickly in his bent-kneed walk.

He looked a little happier as he hurried up to her and told her that anybody was permitted to enter the gates. Many people inside were no better dressed than they were. The man Holme had talked to thought he could probably stay with one of the smiths who traded with the foreign merchants.

As Holme told Ausi all this, he was thinking he was good enough to be his own smith and barter his own work. But he didn't want to live inside the gates. The treetops were visible far beyond the town wall; maybe he could find some place to live there.

When the stranger passed through the town gate, he took the road to the harbor. Many vessels were moored there, gangplanks out, and he boarded one of them. He found the merchant, and they talked for a long time about the situation in the heathen land. The merchant advised him against staying and offered to let him return with him.

Norsemen came and went on the vessel, and the merchant talked with them, sometimes in their tongue, sometimes in his. Many men in this land had traveled widely and could speak both eastern and western languages. The stranger with the gold cross watched them with great interest but with detachment. The cool friendliness never left his face.

The conversation ended when the stranger said good-bye to the merchant and walked back to town again. He looked at the heathens' wooden buildings – well built, many of them with beautiful carvings around the doors. It struck him how quiet this town was compared with those farther south. Without a word, people met each other on the streets; without a word, they listened to the merchants' torrent of words when they offered their elegant goods for sale. A nobly dressed man quietly clipped off a piece of gold from a spiral rod in payment for some cloth of spun gold. Most of those he met looked sullen or morose, and he knew exactly why. They hadn't heard the good tidings.

The stranger had learned as much as he could about the people of the northern land before he came. It was known the world over that they were fierce pirates. The only good thing about them was that they seldom tortured their victims; they killed them swiftly instead. It was said, too, that they did not like to fight anyone much weaker than themselves and that they treated their women well.

The stranger also knew that their gods greatly resembled the heathens themselves: strong, bearded warriors who got drunk on some brew and devoured masses of meat after their battles. And he knew that the Norsemen didn't boast about what they had already done as other people did but rather made promises about what they were going to do. They told about their life's adventures only when they sensed death approaching and then whether anyone was there to hear them or not. Naturally they thought that the battle god heard and drew them to him.

The stranger believed that his tidings would change the sullen faces to happy, gentle ones like his own and that the heathens were unhappy without those tidings. He had no idea that it was the darkness of the endless forests that hung over their faces and the eternal whistling of the wind that sang in their ears. He attributed the presence of so many reddish-blue cheeks to the people's gluttony. He knew little about the winter's chalk-white iron ring around a settlement when the wind died away for a few days or about the wolf's howling outside that was answered by the dogs' anxious barking inside. He knew little too about the cattle bellowing loudly when they heard a snorting bear clawing at the walls of the livestock pen, trying to tear them down.

The Frisian merchant had advised him to find the king and talk with him before doing anything else. Everyone was kindly received by the heathens, and they didn't plunder within their own land. The merchant knew many others who had come with the tidings before, but they had all failed. And the merchant pointed toward a hunched-over carrier who had just walked ashore with a load on his back. He had come many years before on the same errand, but had been a chieftain's thrall for a long time. He never spoke, and his body had become bent. The merchant had offered him a return trip but he had refused.

As the stranger walked up the street, he decided to keep that thrall in mind. An extinguished candle could surely be lit again.

He would probably be a good helper and would know everything about the heathen land.

When the stranger passed the gate through which he had come, he saw the family from the rowboat. The man looked defiant and the woman uneasy as they stood inside the gate. They were beautiful, distinctive human beings, each in his own way, and for the first time he saw that the woman carried a child. The stranger nodded cordially to them, and the woman watched him until he was blocked from view by a building up near the fortress. She thought that the way he walked confirmed that he was an important man.

The guard outside the fortress stopped the stranger with his sword and asked who he was looking for. When he heard the foreign tongue, he called for someone standing farther back in the courtyard.

The stranger noticed that the fortress was a clumsy imitation of fortresses in his own country whereas the buildings in the town were of a kind he had never seen before. He noticed too that people who seemed well off bore weapons from the south and west whereas the others' probably came from the north. A woman walked across the courtyard, her shawl made of the fabric with threads of gold that was such a good item for the Frisian merchants.

The warrior who responded to the guard's call was old and gray-bearded. He could speak the stranger's language, and as they walked into the fortress, he named several places he had visited in the southern lands. He also knew both what the stranger's cross meant and what his god was called.

They passed a long hall full of weapons and benches along the walls. Many men were inside either sitting or lying down. Several game boards lay on a long table. The side of the hall facing the lake contained a series of holes that could be shut up tight with heavy wooden hatches. The fire pit was almost as long as the hall itself, but since it was summer it was clean and filled with fresh spruce twigs.

There was yet another yard to pass through before they got to where the king lived, a smaller yard with green grass and a clear well encircled with round stones. The yard was shaded and cool from the walls on three sides. The fourth wall had a parapet over which you could see the harbor with its many jetties and vessels.

The king could be distinguished from his closest warriors only by the chair he was sitting on. His indifferent glance at the stranger seemed to come to life when their eyes met. There was no imploring or obsequious smile on the stranger's face; it showed the constant cool friendliness that had calmed Holme and Ausi and that had made the wolf in the forest retreat with a snarl. Besides that, the stranger was a stately figure and his movements were deliberate.

The king's broad hand pointed to a chair beside him. The conversation among those close by stopped, and everyone looked at the stranger. The cross on his chest glimmered; most of them recognized it. Many of them had crosses of silver or gold themselves, stolen or copied.

The king didn't understand the stranger's language well, so the gray-bearded warrior translated for them. To the stranger's request to be allowed to teach the northern people about his god, the king answered that anyone could say anything he wanted to. The king himself would like to hear a little about the god sometime. After a couple of questions about whether the stranger thought that additional merchant ships might come for yearly visits, the king ordered a room and a thrall for the stranger. He could eat in the fortress and take refuge there whether the king was present or not.

The old man followed the stranger out and showed him where he would stay. He said that many others had come on the same errand, but most of them had soon turned back. The stranger answered only with a smile, and the old man looked at him in surprise. He wasn't like his predecessors; he was more powerful than they, even though he had come on foot and they in good vessels with expensive gifts for the king.

But when the stranger was alone with the bare gray walls, the table, and the sleeping bench, the strength that had stood by him when he had faced the pirates, the wilds, and the deadly animals abandoned him. Doubts beset him, and he felt powerless before these strong men whose wooden faces were either silent or raging. He lay face down and felt as if his god were far from this land, with little interest in the people living here. He felt an almost irresistible urge to walk down to the Frisian vessel and sail home.

He lay there motionless for a long time, but then as the immense physical exhaustion abated somewhat, his faith began to sing again deep within him. He considered all that had happened to him during the journey, and once again he was aware of a great hand following and protecting him. Among the Master's disciples, there had been a strong man who was occasionally overpowered by cowardice. He must be very much like him.

Soon the stranger could feel the Spirit's power filling his body with a joy that caused him to leap from the bench. He met a pair of sullen, watchful eyes in a bearded face near the door. The thrall had come in silently and now stood there, waiting. The stranger was surprised again. In his homeland, a servant would have bowed submissively to get in his new lord's good graces from the beginning. This one looked as though he'd like nothing better than to strangle him and be on his way.

The thrall held a beautiful bronze dish full of water and a linen towel. He put them on the table, and when the stranger nodded, he went out. But he stayed nearby and no one tried to give him other work even though he spent almost all his time looking out over the endless mainland forests.

From a hole in the long wall, the stranger could see an almost boundless field of large and small green burial mounds among the deciduous trees and realized it was the town's graveyard. From the far end, smoke billowed above the green treetops. He knew that the heathens burned their dead and put their weapons and other possessions with them in the grave. He had come to save them from all such errors or forfeit his life in the attempt.

For a moment he thought about the thrall couple who had given him a ride in their boat. The woman had looked so timidly and wonderingly at him – surely she could be the first to reflect the light. Like his Master, he would go down among the workers and the overburdened – although it would be a great victory if the king could understand and accept the light and proclaim it to his people.

As soon as he attracted some followers, he would build a church. The king would probably give his permission, because even if he remained indifferent, he wasn't hostile. Only after he had a church and a congregation could he start thinking about seeing his homeland again.

Once he had washed himself, a nagging loneliness drove him out again to the harbor to look for the Frisian thrall, but he wasn't there anymore. The ship had been unloaded, so he had probably gone on to another looking for work as a carrier. There was another harbor on the other side of the point, but it contained no foreign vessels. It held only the heathen land's high-prowed ships, with the same kinds of bright-colored animal heads as the pirates had had on theirs.

The stranger walked along the shore until he came to the opposite palisade and followed it upward. The buildings, which were smaller and shabbier, were made of wood and branches and mud. Many children, close to naked, were playing there with small bows and were practicing sharpshooting at a piece of bark on the palisade. Soot and ashes from hundreds of fireplaces were everywhere.[13] The smell of burned bread hung over the entire area.

Farther away, the ground rose to a big hill, soft and open in the sun, and the stranger took a deep breath. The church would stand there – the poor would see it as soon as they came out of their huts. They could come to the church with their troubles and fatigue once their work was done for the day.

The stranger stood in the sunshine on the hill for a long time, imagining the church rising before him. Many curious eyes in the town below watched him standing there, tall and motionless, the cross glistening on his chest.

In their confusion, Holme and Ausi had walked straight through town and were soon standing at the opposite gate. Through it they could see an area growing more and more dense with mixed forest and a few small buildings here and there. The sight drew them on; being on the outside again made them feel they had escaped some great danger.

13. An area of about thirty acres at the center of the Birka ruins has been dubbed 'The Black Earth,' since ashes and other organic materials from human habitation have greatly darkened the soil there. See James Graham-Campbell, *The Viking World* (New Haven and New York: Ticknor & Fields, 1980), pp. 96–97.

To the left, they saw the vast graveyard with its billowing smoke. To the right lay the lake, dotted with fishing boats. A path led toward the huts at the edge of the forest, and they followed it. Cows were either grazing or lying down everywhere. A few horses stood in a clump of trees, their long tails switching.

Many of the small huts seemed to have fallen into disrepair and were uninhabited. An old thrall tending the cows was glad for a chance to talk to someone and told them that anyone could take over the huts. If the owner came back, you just had to move to another. Several had been empty all summer and winter; their owners had gone east or west and never returned.

Holme brightened as he listened to the old man. He felt better there with the woods at their backs. He'd be able to see an enemy approaching from town and take shelter in the woods if he was outnumbered. Ausi was happy too. The town had frightened her, but she was still curious and wanted to know more about it. If they stayed here, they could walk in as often as they liked. Maybe she would see the strange foreigner again and could learn more about him as well. The thought of him made her strangely uneasy. She wanted to be near and serve him so that his clear, gentle gaze might fall on her again, as it had done a few times during the boat trip.

A hut just beyond the first few trees was in pretty good shape. The mud had fallen off, exposing the timber in a few places, and most of the birch bark had come off the roof, but the wood was solid and strong. The door seemed to have had an iron lock once but was only propped shut now. Inside, long benches on two walls met at an angle, where there was a table with a top made of split logs.

The thralls looked around the hut with satisfaction. The fire pit had fallen apart, but an iron caldron remained with its black, splayed legs still intact. The smoke hole was eaten away, crumbling around the edges; some grass and a couple of frail yellow flowers leaned over the edge, looking down into the dark room.

Ausi fixed a bed in the corner for the baby and then helped Holme, who had already started clearing out the room. He cleaned the ashes out and put the stones for the fire pit back in place. A leaky chest with a broken lock and bound with iron bands stood in another corner. Ausi was glad to have it and asked Holme to repair the lock as soon as he could.

The air in the hut was raw and chilly, so Holme brought in an armful of sticks and twigs. There was still some dry grass inside, and soon a fire was crackling and casting its flickering light on the walls. The baby woke up, and her dark eyes glistened in the reflected firelight. For the first time, Ausi seemed to see a smile in the ugly little face, and she told Holme about it delightedly.

Dozens of moths and other flying insects woke from their slumber in the chinks in the walls and began to flutter about the fire in a wild dance. In a couple of places by the wall some little mounds of dirt had been scratched up by forest mice.

Holme and Ausi smiled at each other across the fire. They had never dared hope that things would go so well for them. Holme hung his bow on a peg above the door, thinking how nice it was to have such a fine weapon. It was probably part of the reason for the journey's success. It had certainly helped them be mistaken for freemen – a thrall would seldom carry such a bow.

In several places on the outskirts of town Holme had heard hammer blows that sang in his ears. They came from smoke-billowing smithies, and in one of them he had heard the bellows whistling and squeaking. Holme longed intensely for the smell of coal and iron, for the heat of the hammers, and for the tongs, from the longest kind for taking iron out of the fire to the smallest for ing seams and nails. After he had put his hut in order and fixed a lock for the door, he would go to the smithies and ask around. If only they were in the woods. No doubt the iron had but all come by ship; there was no ore on the island and no bogs – nothing there for a miner to do.

That evening Holme rowed the boat closer to his new home. The lake was almost calm; beyond the expansive, glistening water rose the mainland forests, black and jagged against the sky. He heard a yell from town now and then, a banging door, and dogs barking everywhere. A herd of cows came out of the woods near the hut and ambled toward town, their heads bobbing. Holme rested on the oars, not knowing what he wanted. The woods tugged powerfully and incessantly at him, but like Ausi he wanted to get to know the town a little better – to stay a little while, especially since they had a good place to live. Maybe the smiths here knew more than he did and had better tools. He wanted to find that out most of all.

Small boats littered the sandy shore; he put his among them. A number of them weren't locked; there probably wasn't anybody around who had to steal a boat.

He saw the town wall with its lookout towers in the distance and wondered what enemy they were afraid of. Who could come across the water with enough warriors to defeat the town's defenders? They wouldn't even be able to land; he had seen dense pilings outside the harbors, and only someone who knew about them could navigate a merchant ship to the unloading docks. Of course, he didn't know how far the island extended on the other side. Maybe danger was lurking there.

The fire was still burning in the hut and the air was warm and dry. The moths had stopped swarming and were crawling on the floor, dazed. Ausi had moved the two benches together and had put the skin rugs on top so all three of them could sleep there. After a quiet conversation filled with laughter, they both took off their clothes after so many days of cave life and flight. A little embarrassed, they sat next to each other, letting the warmth of the fire and the coolness of the night dance around them. The baby slept under the skin, her head a little black speck over the edge.

They talked of the distant settlement – of their friends, the grain, and the flax. Ausi wished that the envious women thralls could see her living in a hut she could call her own.

In the silence, both longed for their work and companions – for the smell of the fire, for the pigs, the outlying buildings, the woods behind and the cove below the settlement. The new place, with its mass of buildings and throngs of people, intimidated them.

Before Holme lay down, he propped the heavy table against the door. Ausi lay white and soft on the bench, chewing on a strand of hair and following him with her eyes.

When the first snow-squall came rolling across the cove, the whole settlement was ready. The barn had been stuffed with hay and leaves, wood had been stacked in huge piles, the roof and walls had been examined and repaired. The pigs, still outside during the days, ran, long-bristled and squealing, toward their pen for shelter. The swineherds let them in with a laugh, and they got to stay inside all the time once the snow began falling; during the winter, the thralls fetched them one by one, although they put up a fight, their protracted screams echoing across the cove and ending in a death-rattle. A few drops of blood would be left, enticing the dogs to lick the snow and the magpies to flutter around the area until the next snowfall turned it white and clean. When spring arrived, only the boar and mating sows would remain.

The cows came home from the woods and stood around

mooing for a couple of hours, but when no one paid any attention, they lumbered off again to the trees. At dark, they tried again and were allowed to go into their stable overnight once a little snow had fallen. In the last gray daylight falling through the light holes, the women thralls squeezed the milk from the cold, limp udders.

Both thrall dwellings were empty and dark during the winter. The chieftain thought it unnecessary to heat them, so the thralls were permitted to stay by the door in the high hall. The long fire extended almost that far and kept them warm. The area was divided by a couple of skin rugs hung over a beam, and the women slept on one side, the men on the other of the partition.

The first few nights, a thrall would sometimes try crawling under the skins or a warrior from outside the hall would try sneaking in to the women. But the older thrall women raised a fuss each time, whether to the joy or disappointment of their beseiged younger companions. The thrall or warrior vanished quickly before anyone could see who he was. In a couple of instances of a long-standing relationship between thralls, the old ones remained quiet or enabled them to meet undisturbed in an outlying building or in the woods.

In the autumn, all kinds of work was done to prepare for winter. The hides were cured, thongs scoured, awls and needles sharpened with small slate whetstones. The loom would bang all day; when one woman stepped away from it, another stepped in. Holme had made one weaver's reed out of iron; the chieftain's wife had bartered in town for another made of whalebone.

The women spun flax and wool thread by the fire. They kept an iron or bone spindle-whorl on a rod spinning constantly with one hand, and worked the thread with the other. Each one owned her own spindle-whorl and often had it buried with her.

82

The chieftain's child crawled around by the fire or pulled himself up, groping along the benches for support. He still had to turn his whole body in the direction he wanted to look. The stone had left a hard lump, but on the chieftain's orders, the old woman had stopped her poultice treatment.

One of the younger thralls began to show signs of pregnancy. The chieftain's wife noticed and talked several times with her husband about letting the baby live. Their own child would need someone to wait on him and be his playmate when he got bigger. Finally the chieftain growled his consent. From that moment, his wife saw to it that the pregnant woman got the lightest work possible, and occasionally she would point out the good fortune awaiting the child.

After the snow cloud had passed, a thin layer of snow glittering in the dusk covered the hard, frozen ground. The chieftain and a couple of warriors stood outside in the enclosure, wondering how the winter would turn out. They hoped it would be mild and brief. A long, long time ago, the summers had been longer and warmer.

The sound of thralls and squealing pigs came from the pigsty. It had been divided in two, and the thralls had to keep the animals in the two sections separated. Sometimes a skinny, gray pig, kicked and sent flying, stood still a moment grinning into the cold wind, then returned to the fray. Outside the sty stood big piles of acorns and roots for the pigs' winter fodder.

The warriors urinated on the ground, making the earth peek through again in black, steaming patches. Going into the hall, they laughed at the thralls' battle with the pigs. The long fire burned, and gray smoke hung under the ceiling's sooty beams. Close to the fire, the shoemaker sat with his work. He wandered from farmstead to farmstead, staying as long as he was needed. Neither warrior nor thrall, the shoemaker was widely known and sought after. He brought all the news from town, the farmsteads, and foreign lands.

The skins for winter shoes had the fur left on them for warmth. Around the shoemaker were piles of old shoes needing repair before he started making new ones. A couple of warriors already sat beside him, listening to his talk. After the evening meal, he would be the center of attention.

This time he brought news that another man from the south had come and had the king's permission to stay in town and teach the people to believe in his new god. But he'd probably be driven away by the people pretty quickly or maybe even slaughtered in the nine-day sacrifice – hung up in one of the sacred trees or perhaps drowned in the sacrificial well. It had happened before. As they were all aware, the king had no power to save anyone the people had sentenced.

Stenulf hadn't been seen or heard of anywhere, and the shoemaker was very surprised about his disappearance. He had probably displayed arrogance to one of the gods, and they had killed him in the forest. One of the warriors said that Stenulf had never carried any protection against evil spirits or trolls; maybe he'd had a run-in with them.

The shoemaker hadn't seen Holme or Ausi either. But he had come by land and they had undoubtedly taken the coast route since they had the boat. Sooner or later, though, he'd surely run into them. Probably nothing much had happened to them – they'd just been allowed to stay at another farmstead.

In a partitioned storeroom lay a great many forged iron rods. Those that weren't used at home at the settlement were taken to town on the winter trip. So too with grain and meat if it looked like there'd be a surplus. Sometimes a bundle of cloth, some hides, and various wooden utensils would also be brought along for bartering.

After the midwinter sacrifice, when the sun was strong enough to make the snow on the roof soggy and heavy but not strong enough to touch the ice, everything would be loaded on sleds for the journey to market. The chieftain, his wife, and most of the warriors would go and stay for a few days. The best harnesses hung ready, bronze fittings and chains holding the hames together.

Up until then, there had been no roads leading to the settlement, only a sled path from the lake. Winter fishing was the warriors' only outdoor pastime. Among the barren trees in the grove, you could see the memorial stones with caps of snow on their gray tops. Great swarms of various kinds of birds flew from the forest, looking for spilled grain between the outlying buildings or scouring the garbage pile.

A few snowflakes fell intact through the smoke vent in the roof, creating tiny wet specks on the clay floor. The chieftain's stiff-necked child watched them with interest, poking them. Whenever anyone came in the door, the smoke by the vent went wild from the draft. Large and small iron containers stood by the fire, and an iron-hooped wooden tub filled with clear springwater stood in a corner.

When everything was quiet, you could hear the murmuring waves from the cove through the smoke vent. Toward morning, the blanket of smoke under the ceiling disappeared, and it got colder inside. The snowflakes settled on the floor, glistening a moment before melting.

Outside, snow and darkness, wolves, bears, and wild boars would hold sway for a long time to come.

Ausi hadn't seen the stranger again the whole autumn, but Holme told her he was still in town. He had come to the smithy once to talk to the smiths. They couldn't understand everything he said, but the master smith, who was from the stranger's homeland, interpreted most of it for them.

Holme had heard too that the king had taken up the stranger's cause and was protecting him. Some of the people from town followed the stranger almost everywhere. At his place in the evening, he would talk with anyone willing to listen. A few had even let him pour water on them so they might become like him.

Ausi thought a great deal about that when she was alone all day. How could they become like him? She had heard a lot about the old gods and had seen much sacrifice to them, but they didn't care about women and thralls.[14] From what Holme said, the stranger had more women than men among his followers. That was remarkable and encouraging. If only she knew more about it.

Ausi walked to town a few times while it was still summer, but carrying the child with her was cumbersome and difficult. She also noticed that Holme didn't like her to go even though he didn't say anything. Since autumn had come, cold wind blew almost constantly from the lake, and neither of them had enough clothes. Holme got cold too walking back and forth to town, but he said nothing. Soon he would have worked enough to buy winter outfits for all three of them.

Shortly after they arrived, Ausi saw the three dragon ships with red and white sails steering in toward town. They didn't have the stranger's ship with them. She noticed they stayed for a few

14. Schön, *Fridegård och forntiden*, p. 104, observes that Fridegård could not have found any historical support for his notion of the Nordic religion's being undemocratic. Thor, for example, was considered the people's god. See the afterword to the present volume.

days, but she had no way of knowing that the stranger had also recognized them and, with the king's help, had gotten back a few small items. The ship belonged to one of the men who had fallen, and nothing more was said about it.

The days seemed long at the edge of the forest, and the fire had to burn all day. Holme told of dreadful, evil rumors from town – the sun wasn't coming back; everything would freeze into oblivion. Someone kept daily watch from the tower; people often stood on the rocks and hills watching for the sun. Every day, the air was thick with sacrificial smoke. Many people thought the stranger had angered the gods, and they demanded that he be sacrificed or at least driven away. Then one day, the haze lifted and the sun burst out over dazzling fields of snow. A thousand-voiced shout of joy rose from the town and scared Ausi into locking the door.

From the doorway, she could see the narrow path Holme had forged. It led straight as an arrow to the town wall. If anyone approached on it, she would shut herself in and would not open up, no matter how hard they might beat on the door. Black cargo wagons moved slowly across the frozen lake's endless expanse.

Ausi knew that two such wagons would soon be coming from the settlement; they usually came a little while after the sun returned. Some days she would gladly have gone back to the settlement if only she could have kept her baby and Holme with her. She longed to be there now when the ground was bare under the pine trees on the slope and the snow slid down off the roof, causing the dogs to dash up barking.

But the next instant she would think all was well. If they went back, they'd never get away again. She'd never learn more about the town or the stranger and his teaching. If only she dared go where he talked to people who wanted to listen. They congregated in the evenings after the work was done for the day.

Should she suggest to Holme that they both go? The baby could sleep by herself for a while. No, Holme would never agree. Maybe Ausi could go alone once the evenings got a little lighter. Maybe the stranger would recognize her and talk with her in front of the others. The thought made her cheeks burn with pride.

When Holme came home, he said he had seen their old chieftain and a couple of his warriors. They had come into the smithy to sell some iron, rods that Holme had once forged himself. They hadn't recognized him; they hadn't looked at the smiths and Holme's back was to them. They had had to go on someplace else since the smithy already had enough iron, but the master smith had examined it anyway and had said it was fine, pure iron.

Holme said no more to Ausi, but the settlement stayed in his mind all night. He almost missed it; he had been master there and had had two assistants. No one ordered him around. When work was over, he had always enjoyed gathering with the others to hear about the day. Occasionally someone would show where the chieftain had hit or kicked him, but never Holme.

But when summer came, he would move on with Ausi and the baby. There must be some farmstead in the mainland woods that needed a smith. A man could roam widely there without hearing waves lapping and without always running into the shore wherever he turned. The forest was dark and the moss deep. Here, near town, you never heard a wolf howl, or a fox bark, or wild boars squealing in rage as they fought.

His friends in the smithy urged him daily to move inside the town walls. Didn't he know that only outcasts lived where he did? You had to be an outlaw or crazy. And if the town were attacked from land some night, he would be the first killed and his woman taken away into thralldom or something even worse.

Holme already knew that. But he was more comfortable outside town. Besides, why should anything happen just now? A big assault on the town was only possible during the summer when the lake was open. He didn't care about his neighbors; they didn't bother him and he seldom saw them. Only narrow paths in the snow and the smoke from the roofs indicated that anyone lived in the little huts.

Work was fine, but he always looked forward to the day when he'd be on his own. He was just one of five here, but he wanted to be first or on his own. There was nothing for him to learn in the big smithy; he had done everything before. They made weapons, plows, knives, pots, and frying pans, and he had made all those things at the settlement. He could test out new ideas back there, but here someone else determined every blow of the sledgehammer.

The days in the cave had been the best of his life. He would never forget his happiness when Ausi had taken hold of him and drawn him to her in the cave. But he had gone into the woods so she wouldn't see that; she shouldn't know. He had never dared believe that she, the most beautiful woman at the settlement, with her cool disposition, would be his the way she was in the cave and had been ever since.

He didn't want her walking around town alone. Some powerful man, perhaps the king himself, might see her and force her along with him. When summer came, they would leave, and he'd build a better house than this one in a good forested area somewhere. He'd see to it that he had various kinds of tools with him, and they would own some cows or at least some goats so Ausi would have something to do.

Ausi felt a strong urge to turn back about halfway to town; she was so unused to going alone. Holme had finally given in to her, though hoping she would hear the stranger once and have enough.

It was half-light; the snow had melted slightly in the midday thaw, forming a crust on the surface. The lake was still covered with blue-gray slush, but showed an open, clear black rim near shore where a couple of birds were swimming. A distant flock flew off with a whistling of wings.

Holme had sullenly given her directions. Past the fortress, up the slope, a nice big building with a cross on the door, like the one the stranger wore on his chest, only made of wood. Besides, she couldn't get lost; the stranger had someone standing outside, luring in any passersby. Sometimes he was successful, but once in a while he found himself lying flat on his back. Served him right; he had to learn to leave people in peace.

Heart pounding, Ausi walked through the gate without looking at the little guardroom. She heard the guard jump up from his bench and knew he was watching her, but he didn't call. She wished she were a little better dressed, but it would soon be dark.

Many men met her on their way home, but they didn't even notice Ausi. She felt a little safer passing the fortress she knew was full of warriors. She thought about the people from the settlement, but they had gone home a long time ago. Holme had kept an eye on both their sleds, and finally one day he saw them disappear on the distant ice.

At a distance Ausi saw the building and hesitated again. Two women came up behind her, and she let them pass. They walked purposely straight toward the building, and she followed. A man opened the door and gestured them in.

Some benches lined the wall and others ran straight across the floor. A good many people sat there, and Ausi saw a couple of well-dressed warriors in the first row. One of them had a gray beard and friendly eyes.

The stranger alone sat at a table. His head was bowed, and something rested in front of him. Ausi shivered and her heart pounded. This was both upsetting and delightful. A strange candle stood beside the stranger's head, a kind she had never seen before. It burned noiselessly as though out of great respect for him. How could a flame be so quiet and still?

A few more people came in, and then Ausi heard the man close the door. He walked forward, stood behind the stranger, and waited. The stranger kept sitting there; not a sound could be heard in the hall.

After a while, the stranger rose and slowly looked out over the congregation with a clear gaze familiar to Ausi from the boat journey. In a soft voice, he spoke and she listened without understanding the words. Her head swam, and she wanted to crawl on the floor to his feet. By the time she had calmed down, he was speaking short sentences, and the man beside him translated them after him. It took a moment before she knew what it all meant, but eventually she was able to follow along and understand almost everything.

It was as Holme had said; the stranger's words were even for women and thralls – in fact, for them most of all. Ausi anxiously looked at both the warriors, but they sat quietly, calmly. They didn't knit their brows and stomp arrogantly off even when the stranger clearly said that the first would be last. This was all very odd. The chieftain and the warriors at the settlement surely would have torn the whole building down if they had been insulted in that way.

She saw the faces of the women and thralls light up with joy when the stranger said that the new god demanded nothing; no animals had to be slaughtered for him, no silver or gold buried in the ground. The warrior wounded in battle or the thrall woman sick in the forest – both could crawl forward to the Powerful One and be comforted and healed.

When the stranger had finished speaking, a man rose from the bench by the wall and said in a harsh voice that he didn't believe the stranger's words anymore. Nothing had improved for him even though he had done everything he was supposed to. He had always had bad luck, and he still did. He was leaving and would not return. He might just as well stick with the old gods or have none at all.

The stranger didn't look at the man who spoke and didn't seem to hear him. He picked up the candle and walked among his listeners, saying a few friendly words here and there. All eyes followed him, sparkling with reflected light.

When both were standing in front of Ausi, the stranger looked at her in surprise. She was looking down, and her long eyelashes cast shadows on her cheeks. Her chest heaved under the bronze brooches. The stranger searched his memory and soon placed her. He was glad and took it as a favorable sign that she had come there of her own accord. Her black-haired husband wasn't along, but maybe he would come eventually.

The stranger spoke a few friendly words with his hand on Ausi's head, but she got up and walked toward the door when she realized she might burst into tears at any moment. She couldn't get the door open, but the interpreter was just behind her to help. Just as she went out he said something that she didn't understand. Probably something about coming back another time.

The town was deserted now, and Ausi walked between the rows of silent buildings. She didn't meet anyone, but a fire burned in the guardroom, shining on everyone who passed by. She hurried quickly through and heard the guard get up again and come out. His voice followed her, laughingly suggesting she come into the guardroom with him. He had such a nice bench in there.

The spring night was silent outside town, and the air was mild. The footpath was a dark stripe in front of her. Melted snow trickled across the path in one spot, and when she walked under a big spruce tree, a couple of heavy drops fell on her. She felt the moisture seep through her shoes and spread out under her feet. But she'd be getting new shoes and clothes soon.

It wasn't too dark to see the numerous footprints that had appeared since Ausi had left home. Several times, Holme had walked out about halfway and back. He had been anxious about her and that made her happy. Holme, the baby, and the hut – they all seemed more pleasant and dear after she had been away for a while.

Ausi had wondered if Holme would be gruff and angry, but he was himself. He listened to her story without scorn but also without great interest. He had warm food in the caldron for her – a meaty bone with broth and cooked roots.

Ausi held the baby to her breast with her left hand and ate with her right. She talked, and Holme finally showed some interest when she said that the new god didn't want anything for what he did. That was why he was so good for thralls and other poor people.

'And you shouldn't burn your dead anymore. Someday the new god will come back and wake them, and then you have to be unburned so you can arise. Anyone can understand that . . . .'

'Is that what he said?' Holme asked, getting up suddenly from the bench. 'Don't you think he's lying?'

'No, I don't.'

Holme lay down again pensively. If that were true, then the strange god could awaken Stenulf. Holme had often thought of Stenulf uneasily. He would tell the stranger approximately where he was so he wouldn't be forgotten.

Then the nice, white god could see a real warrior. Holme imagined his huge shoulders shooting up out of the mound, hurling the stones down the hillside. It was good he had his sword with him. The strange god would be glad to count Stenulf among his warriors.

As he thought these things, Holme watched Ausi. She was like a completely different woman; her cheeks were red and her eyes glowed. He felt uneasy again when he saw how beautiful she was in the firelight. He must take care that no powerful chieftain caught sight of her. If only the summer would come soon; then the woods would hide her.

Naturally, Ausi could attend the stranger's meetings again sometime since she seemed so pleased with them. There didn't seem to be any harm in that. She said herself that only a couple of warriors were there, otherwise mostly men and women thralls.

He was glad to know about the unburned being called to life again by the new god. He wouldn't forget to show where Stenulf was.

Ausi was wide awake and excited by her experiences. She told the whole story again, except for the stranger's putting his hand on her head. She had a feeling that might make Holme suspicious. He wouldn't understand how the stranger had touched her. It was like a father's hand she had felt on her hair, yet different. He was so young and tall.

She moved restlessly on the bed, unable to decide what she wanted. Holme lay quietly, perhaps sleeping. Ausi's body was tense and warm; she wouldn't be able to sleep for a long time. If only Holme would take her; tonight she needed the limpness and heaviness that followed. She had been wanting that ever since coming home and the thought lingered, burning.

She raised up on her elbow and looked carefully over his ear and the black lock of hair. His eyes were open, and he looked up with surprise and joy. Their eyes met, lingering and enticing, and then lost focus. Holme had longed for the moment when she would come to him again of her own free will.

The dying fire caught an unburned twig and flared. It crackled, lighting up the room a while longer. By the time it went out again, Ausi was asleep in Holme's rugged arms.

From the door of the hut, Ausi could see the lake grow darker and darker in the sunshine, and one day a warm and strong wind started blowing. The ice rumbled and sang; it shot up on the land in big floes that glistened in the sun as far as she could see. The snow was gone except in the woods, where isolated drifts grew dark with pine needles and yellow birch leaves.

The evenings were light now when Holme came home, and he often looked off toward the mainland forest that rose up dark against the spring sky. Restless and uneasy, he busied himself with his tools and acquired new ones. Once the ice was gone, he worked several nights putting the boat in repair. A couple of friends from the smithy helped him lower it into the lake.

Ausi followed all this anxiously, knowing perfectly well what it meant. But she didn't want to go back to the woods; too much was holding her where she was. She had been to the stranger's house several times, and she now understood more and more of what he said. She had gotten to know a couple of the women, and she longed to see them again and hear their voices. It had been so long since she had been able to talk with other women.

Memories from the settlement and the cave came to her less

frequently now. She had so much to be happy for; here no warriors tried to rape her, no dangerous animals lurked in the forest,
and then there was the stranger. A pack of wolves approached
over the ice one cold winter day; she saw them when they were
only small black dots in the distance. But they stopped, sniffed toward the town, and then ran diagonally past the island toward the
other shore.

It would be good if she could get Holme to go see the stranger
with her. But he wouldn't listen. All he cared about was that Stenulf wouldn't be forgotten if the unburned were truly to rise again
some day. He had asked Ausi to describe to the stranger as well as
she could how to get to the mound.

But she'd eventually get up the courage to discuss her problems
with the stranger. He'd probably know what to do. She didn't con-
sider for a moment staying behind if Holme left, but her heart
sank whenever she thought about the forest that would hide her
for all time.

She saw the group as it passed through the town gate, and she
began getting the baby ready. They were walking along the shore,
and if she took the road through the woods, she would catch up
with them. She recognized the stranger and the old warrior bringing up the rear. Some women were walking in front.

Her new clothes were light-gray linen, and Holme had come
home with two large bronze brooches for them. Ausi carried the
baby in a woolen sack, and as she walked, the baby laughed and
reached for her nose and chin. For a moment she thought of the
chieftain's child and the stone Holme had thrown at it. Ausi still
thought it had served them right – why had they put Ausi and
Holme's baby in the woods? Besides, they could have more children if that one died.

Having new clothes and the familiarity of the stranger's assemblies made Ausi less timid. She walked boldly up to the people on the shore, and everyone greeted her warmly. The women came over to admire her baby. A couple of them had children with them too.

The group continued along the shore a ways. Beyond a point that blocked the town from view, they stopped near a little cove with a sandy bottom and calm, clear water. A couple of ducks flew away, arced in a half-circle, and landed again nearby.

The stranger had already explained what his god demanded from his followers, and everyone thought it was simple. Somehow his god had to be able to tell his followers from the others. With a few words, the stranger called for God's presence, and Ausi looked somewhat nervously toward the edge of the forest. She half expected to see a figure as tall as the spruce trees even though she'd heard often enough that you couldn't see the new god.

The stranger walked into the water without lifting his clothes. When the water was above his knees, he turned around with a smile and stretched out his hand toward the gentle, gray-bearded warrior. Ausi was glad she wasn't first.

The god didn't request much. The stranger bent the warrior toward the water, scooped up a handful of water, and poured it on the warrior's head as he spoke a few words. Then the warrior splashed to shore, wringing drops of water from his beard. As the warrior walked to the grass between the beach and the forest and sat contentedly to watch, the stranger stretched out his hand to one of the women.

When it was Ausi's turn, she handed her baby to one of the other women and waded trembling out into the cold water. She saw the stranger's gentle smile; he reached out his hand and steadied her. Then she felt one arm supporting her as the other slowly pushed her head down. She heard the stranger's voice speak to God with warm intimacy.

Just as the stranger bent forward to dip his hand in the water, Ausi saw a sudden and wonderful sight. The cross he wore around his neck was reflected under her gaze, shining brilliantly on the smooth, black water. Then his hand agitated the water again, and she felt the cool liquid running over her hair.

Afterward, everyone sat in the grass, and the stranger told them as he had many times before that they were all alike, with the same rights as the children of one father. Ausi felt proud to belong to the group and looked surreptitiously at the warriors, but they seemed calm and satisfied. The water that had run off their clothes and down into the sand soon dried, and Ausi felt a slight warmth permeate her wet shoes. A short distance back in the woods, some women stood looking in amazement at what had happened by the shore.

Ausi thought that leaving with Holme would be a little easier now. No matter what happened to her, the stranger's god would be watching and would come to her aid. He kept track of all those who had water poured on their heads, even if they were killed and buried. But she would still prefer to stay in town.

The stranger told them that they would build a house, a temple for the new god. It didn't need to be decorated with gold and silver as he had heard the temple of the old gods was. God Himself shone brighter than all the gold in the world, but He wanted a place where His followers could meet before Him, a place not to be used for anything else. The bare hill above the smithies would be a good place, and surely that was why God had let it remain untouched.

No one spoke, but most of them knew that a great deal of human blood had flowed on that hill. It was an ancient place of execution, so who would want to build anything there? But the new god could do so much; surely He would cleanse and sanctify the hill.

That evening, Ausi let Holme know how much she wanted to stay. With her arms around his neck, she said she didn't want to go to the forests just then. Maybe later. She really didn't know why but she didn't want to go.

Holme answered laconically as usual, but she could tell by his face that he was puzzled and disappointed. He hadn't considered this for a moment. And he shouldn't have to; a woman ought to follow her husband, but just then it was very hard. Ausi was in the middle of something important and had to finish it. She would gladly go later.

From that moment, she saw mistrust in Holme's eyes when she told him anything about the town or the congregation. He said nothing about the baptism; there was no harm in what happened under the open sky. And it was so little compared with what the old gods wanted. He had seen a nine-day sacrifice once.

When Ausi hadn't wanted to go to the woods, he had searched for a reason for the misfortune and concluded it had to be the stranger's fault. Under Holme's low, broad forehead, hatred for the stranger was born and began to grow. Everything was so well planned – the tools prepared, the axes and the spear sharpened, nails of all sizes forged, and the boat ready by the shore. And then this.

Holme realized vaguely that he couldn't drag Ausi down to the boat by the hair. She wasn't like that. She had to come willingly; whatever you took violently from her or forced her into wasn't worth much. He would have to wait.

The stranger had done this evil deed to him, but the stranger was not invulnerable.

Once Holme had made the decision to leave, the town became

dreary. He would sit for hours on a rock, looking east toward the jagged black mainland forest standing against the blue-green sky. He contemplated building a house and owning a smithy that people needing a master smith would seek out.

The baby crawled across the grass, grunted, and lifted herself up against his legs. Holme didn't pick her up, but supported her back with his hand. The chieftain's child stuck in his mind – was it still alive or had he delivered its death blow? He drove the thought away; it was always unpleasant. But the chieftain should have been on his guard.

The summer had just begun; he should settle down, not worry about a trip. Maybe Ausi would want to leave someday. She would probably tire of the new god eventually. He never bothered about such matters himself, but women were different. No god existed who cared about thralls. It was all the same anyway, but if this one could raise the dead, it would be good for Stenulf's sake.

The baby slid to the ground again and crawled away, turning her head right and left. She would soon be standing up and walking; it might be a good idea to wait until then to move anyway. She was getting hard to carry, and if she could trudge along a little on her own, it would be better for Ausi. All Holme could carry himself was tools and weapons, he'd acquired so many.

He hadn't told Ausi what had happened in the smithy when the stranger came to talk about his god – how Holme had winked at his friends and then raised a din with his sledgehammer on the anvil. His friends understood immediately, and four other hammers joined in. A scream wouldn't have sounded any louder than a rat squeak. They reveled in their nasty trick, the whites of their eyes and their teeth glowing in their blackened faces. The master smith hadn't tried to stop them but instead had stood there in amusement, waiting to see what would happen.

But the strange man didn't get angry, and he didn't try to outshout the hammer blows. He had just smiled cordially like that time in the boat, then walked away. When they stopped hammering he was standing in the door saying in a gentle voice that no noise could drown out the quiet message he wished to give them. But he could keep his message.

He got a taste of how preaching to us is, Holme thought, brightening at the memory. Every time he thought how Ausi and he could be in a good place on the mainland by then, starting to build, he felt a passionate hatred for the stranger. If only he had thrown him in the lake instead of rowing him to the island. No one would ever have known.

The stranger had done him a lot of harm, and one day he would repay him. Holme could have dragged another woman from the settlement – any other – down to the boat by the hair, but not Ausi. That was unthinkable.

The fire was burning, the bellows clanging and hissing as the smiths laughed scornfully at the stranger walking out the door. He knew that one of the smiths was Ausi's husband; he recognized the broad cheekbones, the black shock of hair, and the hostile look. It would not be easy to bring a reflection of divine light to those eyes. Of course he was happy about the ones who already followed him, but there were so lamentably few. Heathens were swarming everywhere, unassailable in their strength. He was probably too weak to stand alone in this heathen land, endless and uncharted.

Part of the lumber had already been dragged up the hill. Perhaps things would move more quickly once they had a little church. He had asked one of the Frisian merchants to bring a bell back with him on his next trip. It would ring over the district, calling the heathens to the church on the hill. He must pray for a miracle for them, a great miracle. They would never pay attention to anything else.

The king, who had left town to visit one of his farmsteads, had been friendly and obliging, but he hadn't concealed why. He wanted more trading ties with the Christian lands, more ships loaded with goods. Even so, he did nothing to limit the pirates' ravaging. The Frisian merchants never knew whether they'd reach their destination with life and cargo intact. There were those who claimed the king himself had dragons out plundering.

The darkness the stranger had to conquer was boundless. The blackened, scornfully laughing smiths had made that clearer than ever for him. If only he could walk on board one of the merchant ships and return home. Someone stronger than he was needed here. Or, if that were impossible, he would stay and suffer a bitter but ennobling death by knife or fire.

Only two freemen had joined him; the rest were thralls. And the younger warrior was already wavering, probably tired of the thralls' company and his friends' scorn. The older one stood firm and had ordered the timber hauled up for the church. The hill was free and no one could stop them from building there. They would start as soon as possible and raise it with their own hands – himself, the old warrior, and the thralls. The women would help however they could.

During the summer, he had talked from the hill, with the people sitting in the grass. Many passersby stopped, and the hillside was often gray with people. They sat with motionless wooden faces, concealing whether or not they felt anything in their hearts. He was so tired of these hard, cold people who were never moved, who never cried or rejoiced. They were either infinitely calm or raging beyond measure. There was no singing or playing among the adults and scarcely any among the children. Their poems were long, strange descriptions of bygone events and people who had died long ago.[15]

Even the young girls wore dignified expressions, and the boys played with bows and arrows. More than once a blunt wooden arrow had hit him from some hiding place. No one except the warriors and the noblest women escaped the boys' annoying war games.

Some day he would go to the heathens' temple, a few days' journey away. It had been described to him as glistening with gold and silver and having gigantic statues of the three noblest gods who were worshiped with blood sacrifices; even human beings were slaughtered when the gods' wrath had to be appeased. The third was also worshiped wantonly, both in word and deed.[16] Perhaps there, in the very center of abomination, the Lord's intention for the stranger would be manifest.

However, first the church must be erected so his little brood would have a refuge. A few rows of benches and an altar with the gold cross on it would do. The gray-haired warrior could be in charge if he himself ever had to be away.

15. Since the stranger is a Frisian and therefore from a Germanic, not Latinate, culture, his reaction to Viking poetry seems odd. For examples of the continuity of the Germanic and Celtic poetic traditions, see Calder, *Sources and Analogues II*.

16. The stranger refers to the pagan temple at Uppsala, which Adam of Bremen, the great German medieval historian, described ca. 1070 as being completely adorned with gold and surrounded by a gold chain over the gables. He said that statues of three gods stood inside the temple: Thor, Odin (Wodan), and Freyr (Fricco). Thor, god of the skies and thunder, was the most powerful of the three for the Swedes and was flanked by Odin, god of battle, and Freyr, god of fertility. See E.O.G. Turville-Petre, *Myth and Religion of the North* (New York: Holt, Rinehart, & Winston, 1964), pp. 244–46.

And if he were gone forever, certainly someone stronger would come along one day. Perhaps by then nothing would be left except a legend about a man with a gold cross who had come there once and then was gone. A few had followed him but even they soon forgot everything he had taught them.

All day and all night, the stranger visualized the jeering smiths, and he agonized over his mission. With ravaged face, his cross clutched between white knuckles, he stood on the fortress's parapet the following day watching a Frisian ship putting out to sea and disappearing among the islands toward home.

On the first day of work, they leveled the area and stacked rows of logs chest high. It wouldn't be long before they had their own church. Ausi wasn't there; she didn't dare ask Holme, and the site of the church was too easily seen from the smithy.

Holme had grown more and more quiet and brusque as summer wore on. He no longer talked about moving, but he rowed out for long periods during the evenings, sometimes all the way to the mainland. Many times, he was gone all night while Ausi lay awake, afraid that something had happened to him.

At midnight, three or four figures approached the newly begun church, which looked like a big box in the night. They whispered scornfully about the construction and laughed softly. Holme took the lead, prying loose the upper layer of logs and throwing them down the hill. His friends joined in and soon nothing was left but a jumble of logs at the foot of the incline. Then it was time for the cornerstones; blackened, powerful hands heaved them over and rolled them down the slope toward the logs. Holme wished he had his ax with him so he could chop the corner joints off the logs and render them useless for rebuilding.

The next morning on his way to the smithy, Holme saw the stranger standing on the hill in the sunshine. His god certainly wasn't worth much if He hadn't been able to stop them that night or even put the logs in place again. And to think that Ausi believed He was there, watching everything. He probably wouldn't even be able to wake up Stenulf when all was said and done.

The church builders were reluctant to begin again. They were convinced that evil spirits were responsible for destroying their work. The hill was no good; too much had happened on it; the earth had soaked up too much evil blood.

The stranger had noticed sooty handprints on the logs and stones, but he didn't say anything. Instead he started pushing a log back up the hill. The nearest person lent a hand, and soon everything was in motion again. But there was no speed or joy in the work; most of them were silently dissatisfied with the new god who was incapable of better protecting His interests. The building was for Him, after all.

Every now and then, the stranger saw sooty faces peering out of the smithy. He knew the same thing would happen again the next night if no one kept watch. The first night, he would stand guard himself. He might be able to change the vandals' minds. Or they might kill him. That seemed his secret desire. To die under the bottom layer of logs as the first martyr in the heathen land would be a blessed release. Especially since he didn't seem to be the one destined to spread the light there.

When night came, the gray-haired warrior offered to lend him his weapon if he really thought living beings had torn the building down. Iron was effective even against invisible powers. But the stranger refused; if the cross couldn't protect him, neither could a sword.

He sat on the logs as the sun went down and darkness enveloped the town. Smoke from hundreds of ceilings grew thick, then thinned out again after the food had been cooked. A few women came out of their huts, dumped ashes or food scraps by the door, and then went back inside. The dogs pricked up their ears, snarled, and fought over the morsels. A ship left the harbor, its six pairs of oars rowing toward the mainland. When it passed through a ray of sunlight, the monster on its prow flashed bright red. The boats always sat high in the water as they left town, but they came in heavily laden with iron and grain.

This was a hard and strange land. It was beautiful and luminous, but that only made him heavyhearted. It surely wasn't meant to be inhabited; that was why the people were so hard and contentious. The night was mild and warm, and he didn't need to be afraid of being killed, but even so, there was something ruthless hanging in the air. Maybe he had misunderstood God's voice; maybe He hadn't meant this land whose inhabitants listened only to the language of weapons. Not even the thralls would accept freedom; instead they clung sullenly to their servitude. For a thousand years, the people there had bought their gods' favor with sacrifices, and now no one believed they could get something for nothing.

The stranger needed help and support from his homeland. On the other hand, if he were the right one, his power should grow day by day.

In midwinter when the sun was gone, many had come to him in anxiety. They wondered if his god could bring the sun out again. If so, then they would be willing to sacrifice cows or goats to him. Not even then did they believe that God in His goodness would give them the sun again. When it returned, they forgot everything.

The stranger saw a small boat out on the lake, and he could guess who was in it. It disappeared in the dark water below the wooded point, but it wasn't long before three figures came up the street. They stopped near the new building and once again began to deride it. But they suddenly fell silent, staring at the tall, gray figure striding toward them along one of the long walls.

Two of the smiths retreated to the foot of the hill. The third stood his ground, and the stranger looked into piercing black eyes between two shocks of hair. He recognized Ausi's husband at once.

Holme heard the gentle voice but didn't understand the words. He was angry and confused; he would have preferred the stranger to attack him. He didn't want to back away as his friends had, but he didn't want to listen to that friendly voice.

The stranger put his hand on the heathen's shoulder and in the same instant felt a violent blow that knocked him to the ground. For a moment, he could neither move nor breathe, but he could see the three figures walking down the street. The friends boasted, a little ashamed, about Holme; they hadn't thought the creature coming out along the wall was a living being. Holme scarcely knew himself why his bewilderment had taken such violent form. He had just wanted to be rid of the stranger and his fist had shot out.

The pain from the blow gradually subsided and vanished. Somehow the stranger was glad this had happened; it seemed like the beginning of something. He had been permitted to suffer for his cause. The smell of fresh lumber reached him occasionally, and as he lay there he imagined the completed church. The bell, if he ever got one, would be suspended between two tall poles so it could be seen and so the ringing could be heard far away. The heathens on the mainland would hear it, and curiosity would drive them to the shore. Finally they would climb in their boats and venture across.

It was lovely to lie there, struck down for the sake of the Lord. For some reason, Ausi's husband hated him. God grant that he not take it out on her! It was odd that her husband didn't stop her from attending the meetings. But the women in this strange land often had considerable power over their husbands; eventually she might even win him over and bring him along. He would discuss that with her. She was the best of his women followers, noble and straightforward.

For a moment, his thoughts focused on her beautiful face and shapely body, but he drove the thoughts away at once and castigated himself. What a poor wretch he was, faced with this boundless task. So far, most of what he had sown had fallen on barren rocks.

The stranger got up, his chest still tender from the blow. He could go to his quarters in peace now; the smiths wouldn't return tonight. The church would be finished while summer still flourished.

The thrall who was his servant had made himself scarce after the king had left. He would sullenly bring in a little water or arrange the bed but then would be gone until the next day. You couldn't talk with him; he would recoil, snarling like a dog. Obviously he knew nothing of friendliness and was more suspicious of friendship than of blows and kicks.

When the stranger returned, the thrall was standing by the parapet, looking across the nocturnal lake. The stranger thought he saw a touch of satisfaction in the thrall's eyes. But it couldn't have been that the thrall had missed him; it was more likely that the king had ordered him to guard the stranger's life as his own.

The bed was made and the bronze dish filled with water. The stranger would stand guard again the next night if neither warrior offered to. The smiths wouldn't respect a thrall and the younger warrior had begun showing more and more indifference; he might soon leave the little congregation. The pain of losing one was greater than the joy of finding another.

Soon they would ask for some reward for following him, some proof and compensation. What would he say, what would he give them? They were deaf and blind to the core of his preaching, wanting only to see immediate, tangible results.

The baby was asleep, and Ausi sat down outside with the door open. The day was hot and still; no one was around. The cows sought the hills for a little coolness in the soft breeze.

She trimmed her toenails with Holme's smallest knife as she thought uneasily about him. He wasn't himself anymore; the friendly looks that had given her such joy had become more and more rare, and he never said a word. The expression that had frightened all the thralls at the settlement and made the warriors leave him alone had returned to his face. She'd probably have to go with him into the woods, but maybe it wouldn't be so far she couldn't come back to town occasionally.

Every day she expected the new god to intervene and help her. The stranger said she need only have patience. Either her wish would be fulfilled or something even better would happen. But such things were hard to believe all at once. She'd never heard of the old gods doing anything, even for the warriors, without gifts and sacrifices. And she was just a thrall.

On the side of town away from the lake, Ausi saw a small band carrying a large object through the gate. It must be a corpse since they were heading for the burial mounds. Thick smoke would soon be billowing over the distant trees. She had witnessed it many times and had been tormented by the stench whenever she was downwind.

Almost simultaneously, a lone man walked out the gate on the west side, closest to her. She had been watching the funeral procession, and he had walked a long way before she caught sight of him. She stared, the color rising in her face. It was the stranger, and he was coming in her direction.

Ausi jumped up and ran into the hut. She left the knife lying in the grass, and a couple of tiny flies lit on the handle. Ausi swept the blades of grass and pieces of charcoal into the fire pit and straightened up a little. The iron caldron on the chest was full of water; she quickly looked at her reflection on the dark, smooth surface, and fumbled to redo her hair. Then a shadow appeared on the floor, and the stranger was in the doorway.

Once he started talking, she managed to calm down and even look at him. In his gentle voice, he expressed sadness about Holme's antagonism and wondered if she couldn't do something about it. He surely wouldn't listen to anyone else.

When he had finished, there was total silence except for the flies merrily chasing each other in the spots of sunlight on the clay floor. The warmth and the fragrance of summer permeated the hut. The stranger looked quietly at the woman, having forgotten the rest of what he had to say. He beheld her beautiful face – the long eyelashes, the sky-blue eyes seeking and avoiding his, the chest rising and falling under the bronze brooches. As though in a dream, he stepped closer and put his hands on her shoulders. She stood motionless, looking down at the floor.

Her cloak, hanging loose because of the heat, rustled to the floor behind her. The stranger's fingers trembled as they pulled down the skirt strap from her bare shoulder, causing her brooch to slide to the side and her breast to fall free. It bore a red mark from the brooch but was round and firm. The stranger, trembling from head to foot, took her breast in his hand like a fruit.

A tiny noise from the bench made Ausi turn her head. The baby had awakened and was looking at them with Holme's fathomless eyes. When Ausi felt the stranger's grip loosen, she walked over and turned the baby to the wall. The baby didn't mind being turned, and then all that was visible of her was the little neck and soft hair, damp with sweat, sticking out in every direction.

When Ausi turned back to the stranger, all she heard was a peculiar sobbing noise as he disappeared through the door. He didn't take the path toward town but went toward the woods behind them instead. She walked slowly after him; as he moved out of sight among the tree trunks, she automatically pulled up her shoulder strap and put her brooch back in place.

When she went back inside, Ausi again turned the baby, who looked just as unconcerned as before. The stranger's behavior had surprised Ausi. At first she thought he must have seen Holme coming. Then it really would have been time to run. But there was no one in sight.

She recalled how his back looked as he hurried off – as if he expected to be struck from behind. She hadn't seen men flee very often, even from a much superior force, and he had fled from nothing. Ausi was somehow disappointed but soon realized it was for the best.

Besides, there might be things she didn't understand. She knew the stranger wasn't afraid of anyone. Maybe his god had summoned him from the forest even though she hadn't heard him, and then naturally he had to run. What did a thrall like herself know?

The day seemed so long and warm in the solitude; Ausi would

have liked it if he had stayed and talked a while. He could have sat there on the bench talking with her alone. They probably could have figured out what to do about Holme. Maybe he'd be satisfied and stay if the stranger's god would give him his own smithy.

She went out and looked toward the woods several times, but the stranger didn't return.

Fewer and fewer were helping to build the church, and they worked without any great enthusiasm. Three nights after the stranger had stood watch, everything was destroyed again. The logs lay at the bottom of the hill, and this time the vandals had chopped off the joint pins. If they used the shorter logs now, the building would be smaller.

This time all of them said they didn't want to work there any-more. It seemed clear that either those executed on the hill were at work or the gods had found out what was going on. Most of them thought the new god wasn't very strong if he couldn't protect his own property. If someone had treated the old gods' temple or other possessions that way, his days would have been numbered.

The stranger didn't try to reason with them anymore. He thought about how worthless he was; he couldn't be the one who would build the first church in the world's darkest heathen land. His vision was not clear enough; it had even been clouded by lust for a woman in his congregation. At the last moment, he had been saved by her baby. It hadn't occurred to him until his eyes met those of the child that the mother was a temptation put in his path.

Still, he didn't want to give up; maybe he'd see a sign that would tell him what to do. Maybe, despite his guilt, the highest honor of all was imminent, the Master's way – painful death at the heathens' hands. Already, everyone was talking about the great festival of sacrifice coming in the spring, the older ones with expectation, the younger ones, who had never been there, with curiosity. They never tired of hearing about the festival, which would last for nine days.[17]

The stranger would attend the festival and stare their noblest gods right in their bloodstained faces. Perhaps he would learn the meaning of the call to the north that he had felt so distinctly. It didn't seem to him as if he could achieve his potential here on the island; the power drained from him in the face of the heathens' defiance and ill will.

Maybe he would be the first Christian ever to witness the heathens' great, mysterious sacrificial festival, legendary in every land. After the next snow-melt, it would begin. Until then he would endure where he was.

The stranger had seen a small sacrificial feast the past spring through an open door. It had taken place at a rich family's with its own shrine, and all the relatives had gathered there. They had sat eating around the fire that shone on a wooden image painted with blood, and most of them were drunk.[18] The stranger had stood watching the ritual for a long time, praying for strength to go in and strike down their idol. But time had passed, the men's beards grew tousled, and their eyes shone in the firelight with a wild and repulsive gleam. It would have meant his death to go in and desecrate what they held holy. His courage had faltered, and he had

17. Adam of Bremen describes this festival as occurring every nine years. See Turville-Petre, *Myth and Religion*, pp. 244–45.

18. Turville-Petre explains drunkenness at these ceremonies: 'Alcoholic liquor is a drug; it raises man into a higher world, where he is inspired by loftier thoughts. Its emotional affects [*sic*] are like those of poetry, and that is why, in the myth of the origin of poetry, poetry is identified with the precious mead' (*Myth and Religion,* pp. 259–60). For the myth of the origin of poetry, see Kevin Crossley-Holland, *The Norse Myths* (New York: Pantheon Books, 1980), pp. 26–32.

walked on merely to see the same sight and hear the same uproar repeated in almost every house with a shrine. That night he had felt more powerless than ever before.

After fleeing from Ausi that day, he had sat at the forest's edge until evening, and he saw an old woman walk up to an aspen tree standing in the sun apart from the other trees. She was holding something that she buried in the ground by the foot of the tree. She had barely finished before a soft wind rose, and the leaves of the aspen began rustling back and forth. The woman looked up delightedly and went home, certain that her wish would be fulfilled, whatever it might have been. Then he noticed that the whole area around the tree had been dug up. A fox or a dog had clawed a hole, bringing up tiny white bones from a previous sacrifice.

If he had been the man he thought he was, he would have walked over and persuaded the old woman to forsake that tree for the tree of everlasting life. Instead, he had sat struggling with a passionate, sinful desire to return to the beautiful woman he had just escaped. He could still feel her breast in his hand, and he could still visualize every move she had made as she turned the baby so it couldn't witness what she thought was about to happen.

While the stranger sat in the forest all day, his flesh conquered him one more time. He walked back until he saw the little house, but smoke was coming from the vent, carrying the smell of cooking meat. The shadow of the spruce trees behind the hut fell on it, extending far out onto the plain. Ausi came outside to fetch a bucket of water from the well by the deserted hut next door. She didn't see him and seemed completely preoccupied with her domestic duties.

A moment later, a dark figure appeared on the path, and the stranger drew back into the woods, wondering if the woman would tell her husband what had happened. He didn't discount the possibility; there was something truthful and candid about her. Maybe she would no longer be part of his depleted flock now.

Someday a believer stronger than he would come and perhaps hear about the monk who had tried to clear the way for him. An irresolute monk who had come through the forest, robbed of his possessions but full of faith, whose light had flickered momentarily, then died in the boundless darkness.

That autumn the stranger could already see intense expectation rising among the heathens, and it grew as the winter progressed. It gripped the remainder of his little flock, and soon nobody was attending the few meetings he still held. Some avoided him on the streets; others responded to his words with doubt and scorn.

The looms were pounding throughout the hall, and craftsmen of every kind had plenty to do. Calves and foals with unusual markings were carefully guarded. A great deal of strong beer was brewed and stored in wooden vats that gave it an odd flavor. The usual winter sacrifice was either played down or canceled altogether in anticipation of the big festival.

This winter was milder than the previous one; the ground was bare just after midwinter, and the lake had never completely frozen over. Trade continued briskly as usual. Chieftains and their women required a great many things from the foreign merchant ships that year. Gold-laced cloth, necklaces and arm rings, ornamented swords and knives – all these coveted items were carried back to their farmsteads to be saved for the festival. Like turtles, ships from the settlements came to town loaded down with grain and iron but rode high in the water on the way home.

The king visited the town once during the year. He saw to it that the stranger lacked nothing but remained cordially indifferent to his mission. The king did wonder, however, if he might not need some helpers. If so, they could bring various goods along on the ships then, too.

But the stranger didn't want to send a message to his homeland, and he didn't want to return there. He had no results to show except a handful of thralls still hoping that the new god would give them something or at least help them avenge themselves on their enemies. The old warrior was still his friend but was spending more time with his friends in the fortress than he had before. Only a miracle could open the heathens' eyes now, and he wasn't one who could summon fire from heaven.

The stranger had been completely alone the last few days. His thrall had shown up once but finally had said sullenly that he had to leave for a while. There was water out in the courtyard, and a couple of old women would be home. The stranger could get food from them.

But even as the first few wagons left town to board the ships, the stranger was walking down to the shore to find passage to the festival. He got passage on a family boat in exchange for holding onto a goat during the trip. The goat bleated, staring with terror-stricken, yellow eyes at the waves. Its owners, a middle-aged couple with a nearly grown son who did the rowing, were in a festive mood already. They said the goat was food for the journey; they would live off it for many days. The wife opened a small chest and showed proudly how much bread they had to go with the goat meat.

The man, who clearly realized who was in the boat with them, talked amicably about the festival. He had been to two before, but this would be his son's first. He looked at the stranger's simple attire and said a man could easily go unarmed the whole time. No one would touch him. But on the way home, he should be careful; then he wasn't safe until the beer left people's bodies and they were themselves again.

When the stranger released his hold on the goat and stepped ashore, he looked back. In the distance lay the Sodom of the north, clouds closing in on it, followed by shadows. Numerous boats of various sizes were coming that way. Some people would doubtless travel by water as far as they could; others, those without boats, had to go by land. The stranger was offered a day's ride in the boat, but he shook his head and walked into the forest. He wanted to be alone with his new hunger for pain and death. He walked northeast, and the oarsman called to him saying that if they met at their destination, he could have some of the goat meat.

The forest wasn't as endless and dreary as it had seemed from town. Cultivated glades and clearings were not far apart. The sun warmed the peaceful areas; a boggy patch of ground was completely covered with yellow flowers though the ditch was lined with dirty snow. He could hear horses neighing and cows mooing in the barns. Two panting dogs dashed by, oblivious to him, and copulated farther up on the path.

Beyond the forest, the path fed into a larger road, well worn by both solid and cloven hooves. The droppings on it were still steaming, and off in the distance he could see a group of travelers plodding along. Three or four cows, heads bobbing, followed them. This was the right road; the stranger could even hear mooing behind him where the road came out of the woods. The festival grounds wouldn't be hard to find.

Small clumps of mixed forest dotted the landscape, and there were farmsteads near most of them. At one secluded farmstead, people were preparing to leave, and a couple of cows were already quivering outside the stall. A boy in the group caught sight of the cowbell hanging on the wall, took it down, and started ringing it as he ran around the building. It was a bronze bell with a beautiful, delicate tone.

The stranger heard the distant clanging of bells, and his heart trembled. He stopped and listened. Now there was no sound, now it intensified, diminished, and was gone again. Tears welled up in his eyes – he thought he had heard the same bell two summers ago as he had walked through the forest. Back then, he was walking the road the Lord had designated; since then he had gone astray. He was walking the right path again now. He looked up to heaven, blind with tears and happiness. He hadn't been forgotten; the Lord's eye followed him – He had made an angel ring a bell to give him heart on his journey.

The stranger heard the bell again above and around him. After the boy had circled the building for the third time, the father had gruffly ordered him to put the bell back where it belonged. If the stranger had listened more carefully, he might have heard the man's voice, but his ears were full of the melodious ringing, and he wept, his arm before his face. The heathen land had regained life and meaning; the sun shone down gently, and heaven was bluer than ever before. God had broken His long silence. All was well.

His movements, which had been tired and labored, were rejuvenated, and the stranger felt his old strength come back. The air was alive with singing birds, and the melting snow rippled joyously everywhere. He took out meat and bread and ate as he walked. Suddenly a woman dashed away from a level rock in a field he was approaching, so he walked up to it. There were small indentations in the rock where the woman had laid some fat, undoubtedly a sacrifice to the harvest god. A narrow, well-trodden path connected farmstead and altar.

The stranger walked on, gazing into the heathen land's future. The ringing from the first church's bell would wash away the people's veneration of wood and stone; they would turn their eyes upward, toward the heaven that was clearer here than anywhere else. He knew the day was coming. He was the first indication of it, just as a lone gray bird is a harbinger of spring. His failure seemed necessary now. The Lord Himself had failed while here on earth.

Toward midday, the entire landscape came to life. Wagons, horseback riders, and wayfarers appeared from everywhere, all drawn in the same direction as if by some great force. A couple of times the stranger was offered a ride, but he refused. He didn't want to miss a moment of the most significant walk of his life. A band of riders passed by and a young, arrogant warrior forced the stranger off the road with his little, shaggy horse. The older ones yelled roughly at the stranger, and the band trotted on, their sword hilts glistening in the sun. The leader wore a helmet like those from the stranger's homeland; it must have been bought or stolen there.

When night came, he wasn't concerned about taking shelter or finding someone with a fire. The air was humid, and drops of water were falling from the trees. A thick haze passed before the moon, but there was still some light in the forest, and he cast a faint shadow. A whitened baby skeleton lay near a rock in the woods, the skull no bigger than his fist. One arm lay a few steps away, its tiny fingers scarcely visible. The stranger stopped and asked his god to receive the tiny soul and to forgive those who had left the child to die.

He walked all night and saw many fires surrounded by dark figures. Toward morning he rested at an abandoned camp where the embers were still glowing. A meaty bone, crusts of bread, and other scraps of food littered the ground. A thick bed of spruce twigs by the fire indicated that the travelers had slept there.

When the sun rose and a breeze stirred the gray-white ashes, he got up and continued on his way. The thawing ground had acquired a thin crust of ice from a couple hours of morning frost, but water was gurgling constantly through gullies and crevices. Many of the flowers had closed up, looking like tiny yellow points topping reddish-brown stalks. But out where the forest's shadow couldn't reach them, they were already shining, opened up in the sun.

The day was as clear and warm as the one before, and the area the stranger passed through didn't change much. He had to walk around a little lake, and he got a boat ride across a bigger one. The owner was alone and had laid his ax beside him before rowing out with the stranger. He didn't say anything and didn't respond to the stranger's friendly words. Occasionally the owner glanced anxiously at the cross, and when they reached the other side, he quickly hopped out of the boat. He waited a few steps away while the stranger stepped ashore, then watched until he disappeared among the trees.

Toward evening, the landscape began to open up. The forests turned to groves and islets, the roads improved, and in many places stone bridges spanned the rivers. The number of travelers behind him grew, and the stranger left the road for the fields and meadows to be free of the shouts and taunts. The moon rose behind the spring haze as it had the night before, and campfires glowed near and far. Various signs indicated that his goal wasn't far away.

The stranger consumed his last meat and bread in a crevice. He slept for a while but woke often from the cold. Distant shouts and laughter reached him now and then. He smiled as the cold penetrated his shivering body, but he had no fear of sickness or death. He felt he was being guided and cared for and that he need only walk on with a thankful heart.

The crest of the hill was even with the treetops, and when it grew light, the stranger walked up to it. Before him lay an endless plain, punctuated by pools of clear water. A couple of wooded rises teemed with travelers and animals.

At sunrise, he was still standing on the hill. Far down on the distant horizon the burgeoning light reflected from something. He could guess what it was – the heathens' golden temple. He would be there by evening, and perhaps the festival of sacrifice would begin the next day.

Once he was below the hill he could no longer see the dazzling spot. He set out across the marshy meadows where quacking seabirds were swimming on the pools or flying between them. A reddish-brown animal stood stock-still looking at him, then darted off as he drew near. He saw it melt into the landscape and vanish.

The stranger walked all morning in soaking wet shoes. When the sun reached its zenith, he sat down on the south side of a little rise and took off his shoes to dry in the sun.

He still couldn't see the temple that had glistened on the horizon. The land had grown more forested again and was rising. He deduced that a larger plain lay farther ahead, and from there he would be able to see his journey's – and perhaps his life's – final destination.

The ringing of the heavenly bell had ended his vacillation for all time. Oh, that he hadn't understood the magnitude of his mission earlier! Alone in this remote land, he would suffer death for the heathens' salvation. The bells couldn't mean anything else.

A large group on foot passed at a little distance. There were men and women, but no animals. He thought he saw Ausi, and with terror he drove away the memory of how she looked. Some rough voices wafted to him now and then on the cool breeze that smelled of water, and he suspected the smiths were passing by with their families. A few days ago, they had sent off several boatloads of weapons and iron goods to the big festival marketplace. He had seen many craftsmen moving in the same direction, lugging their wares on their backs – huge living bundles of tankards or other wooden vessels lumbering along on two legs.

There was one last forest between him and the temple. The stranger emerged from it in the afternoon when the sun was going down. From a ridge he saw an almost endless plain, and a river wound and glittered across it from the direction of the temple. As far as the eye could see, boats of various sizes were heading up the river.

He could survey the whole temple area, which was swarming with life. The temple was in the center, but the sun shone behind it now, making the facade lofty and dark. Nearby the ground seemed to mount up in three massive waves. The roar from the throngs of people and the animal noises reached him even across the great expanses.

His courage flagged again as he felt the threats of death accompanying the roar of people and animals like cold rays. He looked into the endless blue for help, his eyes burning. This was his Gethsemane, and he trembled with a feeling of endless isolation. His country, where he could still live for many years, was far away. Why didn't he turn around and catch a ship home? He could do penance there for the rest of his life.

But this was his last battle. No bell or any other outward sign answered him, but when he walked down the hill, he harbored a strength that would not desert him again. His mission had been revealed to him in the clear light; that was his answer, and there was no turning back. He would strike a blow at the heathens' heart by means of their notorious temple, the pride of the north.

In the patch of meadow still before him, no one noticed the stranger. Numerous roads and trails merged here; strange creatures came from the depths of the forest many days' journey away. Wild, bearded recluses – everyone except outlaws – were safe within the sacred area. Deadly enemies met and ground their teeth, but their swords hung at rest by their sides. He had heard it described that way; now he would see it with his own eyes.

He passed an area cluttered with wagons, animals, and people. Farther away were long rows of cases, tables, and chests. That must be the market square. Even at a distance, the temple still towered ominously above everything around it. The facade, with its vertical, rough-hewn logs, resembled a gigantic, golden pipe organ. Next to it was a grove of knotted trees with dense, sprawling branches. A few oddly dressed men moved among the trees and near the temple.

What had resembled three huge waves from a distance were right in front of him now – gigantic mounds of equal size, covered with grass and probably raised by the heathens ages ago. These mounds showed the signs of centuries of wear from feet pounding trails through their yellow grass.[19]

The stranger walked around the temple, examining it carefully. Close behind it grew a clump of small fir trees; from there you could get right up to it unseen. A couple of low hills nearby were completely covered with people.

On the temple's other side, too, were line after line of wagons and animals. Cows mooed continuously, goats and sheep bleated, pigs fought and squealed in the pens. Countless dogs prowled everywhere. The people conversed in shouts in order to be heard above the noise. Beyond the wagons lay a big pond of melted snow, and flocks of ducks, wings rustling, flew back and forth without daring to light on the water.

More groups kept coming from all directions on horseback, in wagons, or on foot. But there were no children; the young people

19. Three powerful Swedish kings of the sixth century (Aun, Athils, and Egill) were cremated at Uppsala, and huge, seventy-yard-wide commemorative burial mounds, now known as Odin's, Thor's, and Freyr's mounds, were raised above their graves. For a detailed account of the excavation of these mounds, see Sune Lindqvist, *Uppsala högar och Ottarshögen* (Stockholm: Wahlström & Widstrand, 1936).

walking around, their eyes hungry with expectation, were full-grown. Only a handful of older women were there but plenty of older men.

The stranger saw rows of huts nearby, but he avoided them and walked toward the wooded area to be alone for a while. The sun had just gone down in the distant forest; this might be the last time he would see it set.

The master smith had invited the other smiths and their wives and grown children to go with him to the festival. Holme balked for a long time. He knew what went on there and was afraid something would happen to Ausi, but his friends' arguments finally won out, and he and Ausi agreed to go. She was happy for the change and immediately began putting clothes and other things in order. The master smith promised to take care of any tax money or sacrifices they might have to leave there. The small children could be left to be cared for by various women for the nine days.

The group went by land and sent their wares and most of their provisions by water. The smiths took beer along and were half-drunk night and day. Even before their arrival, one got punched in the face for trying to take Ausi from the campfire into the woods with him. Holme was never far away, and his friends had to intervene to save the lovesick smith from Holme's rage.

Ausi hadn't seen the stranger again, but Holme told her that no one went to his sermon hall anymore. For a couple of nights the stranger had stood alone staring at the door, but soon it was closed and forgotten. The pile of timber at the foot of the hill grew smaller and smaller as dark figures walked off at night with the logs and took them home for firewood.

In his terse way Holme tried to make Ausi see that there couldn't be anything to the new god. Why hadn't he protected his temple? It could have been finished a long time ago. Could she point to anyone he had helped? He didn't even help his own servant. Everyone had seen him walking around like an outlaw, averting his face even though he lived under the king's protection.

Ausi, who had trembled under the stranger's friendly gaze and hand, wanted to contradict Holme but couldn't find the right words. How could Holme comprehend what Ausi couldn't comprehend herself? He spoke true, but things still weren't as he implied.

Ausi was the only one of the group who had seen the tall, gray figure walking across the fields and flooded meadows far away from the road. She recognized the walk and posture, which was unlike anyone else's. Once again she had felt a curious longing to follow and serve him, to be his thrall. For a long time, she could see him and the flocks of birds taking flight before him.

When he was gone, she looked with aversion at her companions and listened with disgust to their talk. There was something entirely different about the stranger, something purer and better. He should have taught her what it was so she could be like him. Perhaps they would meet there. She still belonged to him even though she hadn't been able to go to his house for a long time. But he had put his hand on her head and poured water on her. She still remembered the way his cross had reflected in the water.

Maybe the stranger's god would appear at the festival and reveal his power. The thought comforted her and she clung to it. She visualized a battle between a huge, fair-haired man and three bloodstained ones. Maybe that's what the stranger was waiting for. It was such a long time between the big festivals. Last time, she had been a little girl at the settlement, but she could still remember how peaceful it had been with only the old people and children at home.

Holme, of course, had been to the festival once, but he never said anything about it. The master smith told him laughingly that Holme was sure to have problems because of Ausi. It was a wild time when the god of the harvest and fertility received his offerings. The most beautiful women were wise not to be around then, when the songs were sung and the beer steamed on the hot stones. They'd see for themselves now whether it would be like the last time.

Soon they could hear the thousand-voiced cry from the animals, and they reached the barrier of wagons shortly after the stranger.

From the hill among the clump of pine trees, the stranger could see the king arriving with his large retinue. No one slept that night, a night aflame and smoky from countless fires. Inside the temple enclosure, three large pyres burned, but from the clump of trees the stranger was unable to see what the heathens had there. He tried to reach the temple once but was pushed back by the throngs of people.

The stranger heard strange and terrible sounds all night. A curious excitement had gripped the seething mass. Sometimes songs flew toward the night sky – a single roaring noise concluding with some shrill cries. The fires shone on innumerable faces around the temple enclosure.

He couldn't complete his mission that night; he couldn't get to the temple. But surely there'd be a more peaceful moment, perhaps toward morning.

Many dark figures walked past the stranger but no one took any notice of him. At dawn the noise subsided, and the densest throng around the temple dispersed, though the area was never completely empty or quiet. People – mostly old people – were asleep on the carts and on the ground around the fires. In the market-place, the merchants began taking out their wares. The stranger saw several who were doubtless his countrymen, probably Christian, but he had no desire to approach them to talk. Still, a thought quickly blossomed, spreading a light within him. Surely the merchants would carry home the story of all that happened here and would speak his name. God's plan for him had foreseen even that.

With this thought, the last trace of depression fell away. His life and struggle would not be drowned and lost in the eternal whistling of the heathen woods. He had been afraid of that, yet had bowed in submission. But now those who came later would hear about him, and it would be a little easier for them. His memory would live on in Christian lands, and maybe in his home district a church would be erected in his honor.

This was the angel in his Gethsemane. How could he have doubted? God's clear eye had seen the sorrow in his innermost soul, the sorrow that all was for naught, and He had sent witnesses to what was about to happen.

The stranger wandered around the marketplace a few times and heard his language spoken among the merchants. He managed to overcome the temptation to converse with them and tell them his name. It wasn't his place to intervene in the plan.

The sun rose and the temple gleamed red and yellow. From where the stranger stood he could make out three gigantic figures in the darkness of the hall. In the grove, many temple attendants were busy tending the tree regarded as holy. Today the festival of sacrifice would begin; everything that had happened during the night was merely preparation.

The stranger was one of the thousands forming a wall around the temple enclosure as the sun reached its high point. Closest to the temple were rows of benches where the land's noblest men had taken their places.

Everything happening before him seemed unreal, like a dream – the huge temple with its three gigantic gods standing in front of him now, the quivering animals who were to be slaughtered and whose blood was caught in large round tubs, the strange songs and ceremonies. He watched the king step forward, dip a branch into the blood, and smear it on the images of the gods. The throng stood in silent expectation, but he sensed they were waiting for something else, a climax. Rumor of past festivals and the stifling feeling in his chest told the stranger what was to come.

He didn't see the major offering appear, but it was suddenly standing there, a tall, young man, ashen-faced but calm. The people around the stranger began breathing heavily, restlessly shuffling their feet. An ornamented bronze container was brought out so that none of the noblest offering's blood would be lost.

As the knife was raised, the stranger dropped his head and stared at the trampled yellow grass under his feet. He couldn't watch what those around him strained not to miss. He whispered to his god, 'You who watched over the thief, take this wretched heathen to you too.' He didn't hear a scream, just a soft flowing sound mixed with the hiss of breathing around him.

Suddenly the silence was shattered as a shrill voice sang a few notes. A mass choir responded, and as the antiphon proceeded, he saw the king step up to the place of sacrifice with branch in hand.

The stranger pushed himself away through an impatiently grumbling and glowering crowd. He wanted to escape the atmosphere and the smell that made the heathens' nostrils flare and their eyes burn. Those gathered farthest away had dragged different things up to stand on so they could see, but the market square was empty. The sun shone on burnished weapons and white-wood household utensils. Water glistened on flooded patches of land in the distance.

In the afternoon the stranger approached the temple again and saw the heathens preparing great masses of meat. Large pieces strung on iron spits were rotated over the fires by two men. Beer tankards formed long rows on the tables. Now that the crowd had thinned out, he could see many of the kingdom's noblest men in their glittering garments and weapons. Beautiful, smiling women, fair-haired and dark, with jewelry glistening in the sunlight, moved, smiling happily, among the men.

The morning's sacrifices were hanging in the sacred trees: one animal of each kind, from horses and cows to sheep and chickens. By the temple, in a tall tree with strange foliage, the man was hanging in a leather sling, and the soft breeze twisted him around so the stranger could see his young, white face, its eyes closed fast. The three blood-smeared gods looked rigidly out across the place of sacrifice. Two of them governed battles and victories, the third, harvest and fertility. The nine days' sacrifice would bring victories and good crops for nine years to come.

It was dark before the moon rose, and no one noticed the stranger sneaking behind the temple. The crowd, dull with fatigue, was eating, resting, and sleeping in expectation of the next event in the festivities.

Under his arm the stranger carried a bundle of dry grass and dry resinous sticks he had taken from a wagon. He crammed the bundle against the temple wall at a place where a stone prevented the end of a log from penetrating the earth. He struck a flint and soon a spark caught hold in the grass, blew up in a gust of wind, and caught fire. The oily sticks began burning fiercely, emitting black smoke, and the stranger fanned out his robe to hide and protect the fire.

A moment passed; then, pleased, the stranger saw tongues of fire licking the logs. The reddish substance smeared on the walls seemed to burn easily. He heard voices close by, but no one yelled or grabbed him.

Then suddenly he heard a muffled cry followed by an uproar inside the temple. The temple attendants, seeing the smoke force its way in between the logs, had sounded the alarm. Soon they came rushing from both directions to find the source of the smoke.

The stranger defended his fire as long as he could. He saw the heathen faces drawing near him, puzzled or threatening. He pushed away those trying to cast themselves over the fire and for a while managed to fend them off. But then a loud, commanding voice was heard, and some warriors threw themselves on him; their iron grip on his arms convinced the stranger that further resistance was futile.

To his sorrow, the heathens soon extinguished the fire. They came running with pots and wooden buckets and threw water up the wall. Soon only a singed spot was smoking.

No one struck or insulted the stranger, and he suspected it was because the protected area shielded him. The warriors handed him over to some of the temple attendants and ordered them to watch him carefully all night.

The stranger was thankful they didn't tie him up. He was made to sit on one of the front benches in the temple, surrounded by his mute guards. The moon rose, big and round behind a comb of forest far away on the plain.

The rumor of his deed spread, and group after group came by to look at the stranger. Most of the people pretended to be just passing by and looked at him without stopping. No one abused him. A dog came up, sniffed him, and stayed for a moment, its bushy back level with his knees. Suddenly it noticed something out in the murky moonlight on the plain and rushed off.

The temple stood before him, the facade's gigantic vertical logs giving it a massive stature. He hadn't succeeded in destroying it, but that was already troubling him less. He had given all to his Lord and thought that perhaps He had other plans for the temple. Maybe it would be destroyed when the heathens were converted.

Once during the night, the stranger's guards fetched bread and meat. They picked out the best for him, and he ate greedily while he marveled at them. There was something magnanimous about them even though they were heathens. They didn't torture anyone for the pleasure of it, and they stood by their word. They would be a great people once the light had spread among them.

The sacrificial grove, hung with dark carcasses, stood in the dark haze of the moon. A few servants walked about protecting the carcasses from the dogs that were prowling and sniffing everywhere. The stranger had heard that the victims would hang there until only bones remained. Huge flocks of scavengers would descend on the grove all during the first summer, and their calls would be heard for miles.

The stranger sat listening to the different sounds of the night. Even now he could distinguish the dull roar of the crowd, and once the furious shrieks of cats fighting cut through it. That, in turn, was drowned out by the dogs barking wildly, and a clamorous hunt started across the field toward the pine trees.

The moon rose quickly over the forest but inched slowly across the sky now, surrounded by a ring of haze. The stranger's guards exchanged words now and then about the festival or themselves, but never mentioned him or his fate. Through the darkness, they glanced furtively at the gold cross glistening in the moonlight, the cross that he held to his chest all night.

At dawn, the stranger saw the moon pale and seem to lift. Out on the bogs, gulls screeched shrilly at the rising sun, and the crows answered hoarsely from the pine trees. The heathens put new wood on the fires and cleaned up around the temple. People cold from the morning came from every direction to warm themselves after their few hours' sleep in the wagons or between skin rugs on the ground.

The king's first glance at the stranger was troubled and full of reproach but betrayed no recognition. He ordered him taken to the assembly place, then walked there himself, surrounded by his top men. The crowd rushed after him, streaming in from everywhere.

Some other prisoners were awaiting sentencing, but the stranger was brought up first. A ring of raised stones stood around him. Someone spoke his name and described his activities up to the previous night. The voice ended by censuring the king for permitting the stranger to work against the gods, provoke them, and thereby bring calamity on the land and people. Even as he spoke, he was interrupted by a roar of agreement.

The king made a speech to defend himself. He pointed out the important trade connections with the stranger's country and stressed how little harm a single man could do. The king didn't believe for a minute that the gods had noticed his presence, and besides, he himself had seen to it that the stranger's activities would come to nothing.

The prosecutor's next speech dealt with the stranger's attempt to burn the temple, their pride and joy, the dwelling place of the gods, and so draw irremediable harm over the land. Many signs during the night indicated that the gods were incensed and that a prompt sacrifice was necessary to appease them. The human sacrifice of the day must be the stranger; the gods surely wouldn't accept anyone else.

The stranger heard the uproar around him, loud screams and thumping. He heard the king try to save him, suggesting instead that he be driven away as an outlaw, but that prompted an even greater uproar. The crowd was adamant, and the king had no power over it. In response to a general, threatening demand, he decreed that the stranger would be sacrificed to satisfy the gods he had angered. The guards bound his hands with a strap, and he was taken back to the temple.

While he awaited the king's return from the judgment place, the stranger watched the heathens putting everything in order for the day's sacrificial feast. Various kinds of knives were lined up on a table, and he realized that each separate sacrifice had a special knife, of a particular size and appropriate design. The sun was already getting warm, and when it reached its peak, the stranger's last moment would be at hand. A heathen would be allowed to live, the one whose place he was taking as the day's sacrifice.

His eyes were drawn to the row of knives, but he focuse instead on the sky where a veil of clouds passed slowly toward the west. He longed for a new sign that everything was as it should be. He was already oblivious to everything around him, and he saw the three idols in the pillared hall as if in a dream vision.

A thought still tormented the stranger. Would he be forced to be the day's final offering, to live and witness the whole terrible slaughter as columns of animals were slowly drained of their blood? He prayed they take the human being first that day.

The crowd was gathering, and the noblest ones were already beginning to take their places in the front rows. There was a light cool breeze, and the women had shawls with golden brooches over their shoulders. An occasional raw, musty odor floated on the wind from the sacrificial grove.

A great fatigue overwhelmed the stranger, and he longed for the moment to come. He understood that this was God's answer, and he drove away every thought about himself, his land, and his relatives. The past was the past; he was standing at the gate now, tired of wandering. Soon the gate would open.

After the king arrived, the temple attendants took the stranger to a spring and splashed water on him. He got to stay there while the animals were led to the slaughter. The stranger didn't look in that direction often, but he could hear the horse resisting violently, almost breaking away from its tormentors.

For a terrible moment, he told himself there was nothing other than what he could see before his eyes, no God, no meaning, no life after the slaughter of his body. But the thought passed instantly when his destination was revealed to him. Who had guided him, who had saved him, who had sent the celestial bells when he teetered on the verge of doubt? He prayed that his faith would persist until the end.

When the moment came, the stranger was led out. Only one knife was left on the table, the most beautiful. The king stood there, splattered from head to toe with blood. Blood stained everyone nearby, and the gods had been smeared again and again with blood. Never once turning to the stranger, the king stood with the branch in his hand.

The stranger watched the golden bucket being brought closer but felt no terror. He prayed only for strength to endure patiently and to show himself worthy of his great predecessors. The surrounding crowd stood completely still. A white feather came floating on the wind, got stuck in a pool of blood, and swayed slowly, trying to free itself. In the next moment, the stranger felt himself seized and lifted by strong hands, carried a few wavering steps, and laid on a bench. He felt his upper body being exposed, and the sun shining directly in his eyes blinded him.

The stranger focused all his force of will and all his strength around a single thought: the nails that were driven through the hands of his Lord and the spear in His side. The stranger hardly felt the knife. The sun just faded away; soon he could look right into it, and he seemed to be moving toward it. It was transformed into the eye of God, and he felt secure because that eye forgot no one and would never be closed. It drew him on, and he was almost there when the motion changed into a gentle rocking darkness to which he gladly surrendered, a darkness filled with sunlight and hope.

The king tried to avoid dipping the branch in the golden bucket; he asked his top man to take his place, but the fierce grumbling from the crowd forced him to perform his ancient duty. The foreign merchants who had managed to force their way forward were astounded to see that the king was merely the people's obedient servant.

The large wooden statue stared lifelessly into space as the king smeared it with the stranger's blood. The multitude felt relieved; the god had to be pleased with the sacrifice. It would give them victory over their enemies, the grain would grow dense in the fields, and the animals would produce offspring in abundance.

The temple attendants brought forward the stranger's gold cross, which they had been able to tear from his hand only with great effort. The king took it and, after consultation with his closest advisers, hung the cross on the chief god. The king and many of the warriors understood what it signified, but the masses thought it was a differently shaped hammer and murmured approval.

The Frisian merchants had already returned to the marketplace, unaware that the day's human sacrifice was one of their countrymen.

The cross gleamed in the afternoon sun, but the stranger hung with closed eyes in the sacrificial grove's most sacred tree.

Even before nightfall, Ausi had tired of the festival. The first few hours were dreamlike; she had never known there were so many people. But they had pushed their way through the glistening armaments and gray hoods of thralls until she was fed up with everything. They could see nothing of what happened by the temple.

She wished Holme's iron hand would let go of hers a while. He had dragged her along all day in a firm, mistrustful grip, and his look was ominous. She hadn't seen what prompted him to do that – the lustful looks of the men they met, their deliberate pressing up against her in the crowd. Ausi's thoughts were mostly on her baby; she wondered if the woman they had left her with was feeding her properly. Sometimes she wondered if they would run into the stranger. But he was undoubtedly closer to the temple with the most distinguished people.

At night after the crowds had dispersed, they walked to the temple. The first day's sacrifices hung in the grove, but a guard kept them from moving any closer. Ausi looked at the three gigantic gods and wondered how the stranger's god could stand up against them. But the stranger had said his god was the most powerful in the world.

If only she could see him there. He would probably be surprised to see her. If Holme would let go of her hand for a while,

Ausi would go look for the stranger. But he held her so tightly that her arm went numb. She almost hated him for that. No one else had such a grip on his woman, and no one else glared around so fiercely.

At night they shared camp with the master smith and his friends. A few of them teased Holme about his bad humor, and one took out a couple of silver articles and offered them in exchange for Ausi for the night. Holme was furious and growled a warning of what would happen to the man after the festival.

All night, Ausi remained locked in Holme's grip and every now and then he made sure that none of the others had come any closer. She lay thinking of how to escape, if only for a little while. She would try the next day. Holme's dark glance and the fierceness of his hold made her weary of everything.

Ausi heard vague reports about what had happened the day before – about an attempt to burn down the temple, about someone's trial and death. She felt a nauseating fear that it was the stranger. So his god hadn't helped him and wouldn't help her either. The good that the stranger had talked about would never be; everything would remain the same.

Holme was pleased and grunted contemptuously about the stranger and his god. He hoped Ausi's restlessness would vanish with the stranger and that when they got home he wouldn't have to watch her standing in the doorway looking toward town several times a day anymore.

Holme had no respect for the three idols either. While an anxious Ausi gazed at them in wonder, he gave them no more than a cursory glance. He'd always been told that they didn't bother with thralls, and he returned the favor. Deep in his rebellious heart something told him the images were nothing to fear.

The second day passed; Ausi still was not able to find out which foreigner had been sacrificed. At camp that evening, the master smith said that if the festival turned out as it had nine years ago, then the third day would be a happier one – a day of offerings to the harvest god, who provided grain, babies, calves, foals, and eggs.

'A man can't be as careful and stingy with his woman on that day as you are now,' he said to Holme, laughing. 'Otherwise, he can stay away. That god likes everyone drunk and happy.'

Ausi heard the master smith's comment without really understanding it completely, but she hoped something would happen. One of the smiths lay red with fever by the fire and couldn't get up; sometimes she wished it were Holme.

The third day passed much like the two before, but instead of thinning out at dusk, the crowd around the temple grew even more dense. Holme and Ausi came along in the wake of a large group of warriors who ruthlessly pushed their way ahead, followed by their women. When they could look around again, they were standing in front of the temple.

Ausi saw more meat than she had ever seen before. Huge slabs turned on spits over the fires or simmered in caldrons. Beside them lay piles of meat, spitted and ready to roast. There were enormous vats of beer, and long rows of beer tankards were lined up on the tables.

The people standing closest were all nobly dressed, and Ausi looked at them anxiously. But no one seemed to notice that Holme and she wore humbler clothes; everyone seemed excited about what was happening in the temple enclosure. The king's place was still empty, but there were good indications that he'd soon be coming.

The image of one god had been moved in front of the other two. The god in front glittered with gold, and around its neck hung a wreath of yellow and blue flowers from the muddy field at the sunny edge of the forest. This god was unlike the two gods of battle; his body was almost feminine and his mouth was turned up in a smile.

The mood was lighter and happier than it had been the past two days. An accidental push or shove didn't bring about angry looks and words. Here and there, you could hear laughing and joking, always about the same thing. The air became more and more charged, and the god's smile reflected itself a thousandfold on the faces before him. The sacrificial grove, its three-times-eight ornaments hanging motionless in death,[20] stood out against the blue-green spring sky.

Ausi saw a huge number of attendants arranging a half-circle around the temple for a gigantic meal. They brought tables and benches for hundreds from a storehouse between the buildings and the grove. They put large baskets of bread and clay plates for the meat on the tables. The beer tankards were lined up in rows, but golden drinking horns glistened at the king's place and a few others.

Ausi caught a glimpse of the king and queen through the people standing in front of her. The king was a tall man, somewhat stooped, with a pair of good eyes peering out from under his golden helmet. The queen was very young and seemed delighted with her beautiful garment. A group of expensively dressed women and men crowded around them.

The crowd moved forward and Ausi wasn't able to see when the king signaled for the meal to begin. But when a couple hundred-people sat down near the temple, Ausi got a better view. The king

20. Adam of Bremen reports being told that a total of seventy-two sacrifices are made during the nine-day sacrifice. See Turville-Petre, *Myth and Religion* p. 244.

and queen had higher seats than the rest and could be seen over the entire area. The god stood smiling in the glow of the fire at the front of the temple. The eating and drinking had already begun.

Those in the back row or standing weren't forgotten. Smoking caldrons of meat were hauled around on poles, followed by bread and beer. Many got what they wanted for themselves at the front of the enclosure. The temple attendants joked, laughed, and passed out things from huge stockpiles. A cheerful, friendly mood spread through the crowd. Friends and strangers talked, clapped each other on the back, and drank to each other. They no longer paid attention to differences in clothes or station.

Holme and Ausi hadn't sat down when they had the chance, so they had to stand in the first group of people behind the tables. New fires flared everywhere; anyone was welcome to sit by a fire. In front of the god's feet, beer was poured on hot stones as an offering; at times the god was completely hidden by steam from the beer. Smoke hung over the entire area, and the moonlight went unnoticed although it forged broad yellow paths through the distant melted snow.

Ausi was chewing on a fine big mutton bone with meat on it. Holme had brought over a beer tankard, and Ausi took a couple swallows of the strong, bitter, and frothy beer. Soon she grew animated, laughing at everything she saw and heard. Even Holme bared his teeth in an occasional smile though his eyes never lost their vigilance.

As far as the eye could see, fires were shining on rows of laughing faces or dark backs. The thralls, driven by curiosity, daringly wandered far in among the chieftains' tables, but no one chased them away. Drunken and smiling, the temple attendants kept dragging out more food and drink, more wood for the fires. At the marketplace, a few merchants were selling mead, and a great throng surrounded their table. The god stared out over his people, smiling.

Strangely dressed people began gathering within the temple. The people turned around in their seats so they could see into the temple. The murmuring quieted down, and you could hear the fires crackling. From the darkness beyond the fires came loud, drunken laughter.

The singers gathered around the god, and the crowd fell completely silent. A man's loud, clear voice began singing, and Ausi listened, half-dazed. But what she heard couldn't be possible! What male thralls talked of only when they didn't think there was a woman around the man was singing about in front of everyone. You just didn't sing about such things! Everyone joined in; then the voice was alone again, still describing all that could happen between a man and a woman in private.[21]

Ausi's cheeks flushed, but she couldn't keep from listening, soaking up every word. She was aroused and transported. She heard heavy breathing around her, and when she turned, she met a forest of eyes glistening in the firelight.

The singer stopped, replaced by another who sang a different song but described the same things, even more blatantly. The song thanked the god for the pleasure and enjoyment he provided and carefully described how he should be honored. When certain words were repeated, everyone raised a tankard.

Among the long rows of silhouettes, Ausi could see men and

---

21. Schön, *Fridegård och forntiden,* p. 109, points out that Fridegård found the detail about obscene songs being sung in honor of Freyr Helge Ljungberg, *Den nordiska religionen och kristendomen. Studier över det nordiska religionsskiftet under vikingatiden* (Stockholm: Hugo Gebers förlag, 1938), pp. 261ff. Schön shows that Ljungberg's book was one of Fridegård's major sources for his knowledge of Nordic religion. See the afterword to the present volume.

women edging closer together. Hands sneaked into secret places; legs sought each other under the benches at the song's arousing words and melody. A man on her left grabbed her hip; Holme didn't notice, and Ausi stood absolutely still. It was a kind of revenge for the firm grip on her right. She looked furtively at the man, who was tall, but young and beardless.

The singing continued, but something else was in the air. The singing vanished into the temple, and the attendants put more wood on the fires so that the whole area was lighted up. Two people, a man and a woman, emerged from the temple. Both wore only light skirts and were the stateliest figures Ausi had ever seen. She felt both Holme and the other man tighten their grips on her hand and hip. A murmur like the squall of a storm rose among the crowd and fell as fast as it had risen.

The man and woman performed a dance, revealing enough of what the skirts hid to drive the crowd wild. Ausi was burning with a flame that had to be quenched. She resented Holme's hold more and more and pressed harder against the unknown man's hand. People behind them forced them forward a couple of feet, but neither man let go of her.

The dance of tribute to the fertility god ended with the beautiful couple partially blocked from view behind his effigy. There they enacted, actually or symbolically, something that made the crowd boil and surge like a forest in storm. The crowd could catch only rapid glimpses of one or the other's movements and then finally the woman's head on one side, cast back, flower-adorned hair hanging down. The god's body concealed the rest, and he grinned as if in mute empathy with the spectators.

Ausi felt Holme's hand trying to drag her away, but she struggled defiantly. The other man was now holding onto her arm. Then, like a wedge, the crowd behind them came with brute force between Ausi and Holme. She felt his fingers clutching at her fingertips, desperately trying to hold on. The next instant there was nothing but a flood of strangers where he had been a moment before.

Without a word, the man plowed through the crowd with her. She followed, drunk with the beer, the song, and the spectacle. Soon they were beyond the press of people, and Ausi could see a dark clump of pine trees rising from a moonlit plain. The man pulled her into the blackness, swept her into the air, and dropped with her to the ground.

Hard roots and stones under Ausi's back joined with the couple in their tribute to the god. The lust, like rivers ready to burst their banks, had swelled for hours, and scarcely had they imagined the possibility of release before they threw themselves into each other's arms and were united. When their passion ebbed it was replenished once more as if from a hidden spring. Ausi heard voices and laughter nearby but neither could nor would move.

She was still in the ebbing throes of passion when the man disengaged. Surprised at her beauty in the moonlight, he stroked her clumsily on the cheek. He was young and awkward and once his warrior body had spent itself, he left her without a word.

Ausi felt the cold rising through her clothes but was still too weak to get up. She didn't think about anything, but wished she could stay where she was and sleep. The dull roar of the festival seemed far away and unrelated to her. A few couples hurried by, breathing heavily.

She sensed someone next to her and sat up. A man with a long beard was kneeling beside her. Grinning, he put his hand on her breast to push her down again.

Disgust and rage gripped Ausi, and she hit the man hard enough to knock him off his feet. When he got up again, she was already running across the moonlit plain. Before she reached the temple area, she stopped and straightened her clothes. She had dark wet spots on the back of them, but she saw many other women who were wet and muddy too.

Ausi was constantly accosted by drunken men and had trouble getting free. She tore herself from the roaring crowd again and walked toward the smiths' camp. No one was there but the sick smith who, red with fever, had rolled himself closer to the waning fire. His teeth chattering, he said that Holme had been there twice and had gone off again.

Ausi put more wood on the fire and warmed some beer for the sick smith. Then she lay down between the skin rugs and smiled contentedly. There was a smell of fresh pine twigs; she saw the moon swaying in the smoke above the fire and heard the distant uproar and shouting before she fell asleep.

Holme didn't wake her when he came back the third time. He had charged through the crowd in every direction, enraged and worried. A woman seeing his dark, grim face reached for him even though someone else already had an arm around her. He saw couples hurrying off into the darkness, and he searched all the more frantically for Ausi.

When he saw she was asleep, Holme sat next to her, staring quizzically into her face. It was calm and innocent; nothing could have happened to her. She hadn't been separated from him for long; they'd probably just kept missing each other in the crowd.

The fourth day was like the first two. It was the supreme battle god's second day, and fresh blood flowed; new sacrifices were hung in the trees. The wind blew hard, and the bodies swung back and forth, the large ones ponderously and slowly, the small ones rapidly. The scavenger birds flew screeching into the storm or sat quietly in the pine trees.

Ausi saw the stranger again that day, and she wept softly into her arms until nightfall. No god cared about women and thralls after all; the stranger had been wrong. Or perhaps he had fallen into disfavor with his god, and who could survive that?

On the other hand, the stranger's god might have been there and been powerless to help His servant against the three massive gods in the temple. They had to be powerful and dangerous; anyone could see that. Huge and motionless, they stood there glistening with gold and blood. One of the wooden gods wore the stranger's gold cross around his neck as a token of victory. He held a big silver hammer in his hand and someone next to her told Ausi he was the mightiest of the gods.

The sixth day belonged to the fertility god once more, and the scenes of the third day were reenacted. Holme was already dragging Ausi away when the songs started. He didn't drink any beer that day and didn't let Ausi have any. They sat in camp, listening to the murmuring rise and fall. Anxiety and sorrow filled Ausi's heart, and she longed to mingle with the crowd and escape everything, to frolic and be seized by unfamiliar hands. What did it matter, now that all she had hoped for and been happy about was gone forever?

The sick smith had died and was lying under a skin a short distance from the fire. The next day his body would be burned in a place set apart for the ones who weren't taken home after they had died or been killed during the nine-day sacrifice.

On the ninth day, the smiling god's last, Ausi had disappeared by noon, and Holme couldn't find her. Strangers brought her mead and meat; she heard new songs and once again saw the beautiful couple, who were even bolder now than on the first day. With flushed cheeks Ausi witnessed everything the couple did behind the god and felt an intolerable burning inside as the steam, rising from the sacrificial beer, obscured them.

She drank more beer and sweet mead, was led away, and was soon oblivious to everything that was happening. She must either really have been inside the temple or had she dreamed of a soft, red lair and half-naked people, men and women wantonly joined? Hadn't the handsome priest of fornication who had danced around the god come and lain with her even though many beautiful women were tugging at his clothes?

Someone helped her past the three gods in the dawn, and for a moment she caught the terrible smell on a wind from the sacrificial grove. Then she found herself wandering around the marketplace where the merchants were gathering their remaining goods together and getting ready to take them away.

Ausi's head gradually cleared, and she saw people leaving in every direction. No one looked at her; the men were sullen and cross as they arranged things for the journey, and the women were officious. Everywhere people were collecting their things, and in one place two women were arguing over a bronze dish.

Suddenly Ausi was gripped by a strong desire to be away from it all, home with her baby. Today they would begin the return trip; she must go to the camp. The ground was well worn everywhere, and it looked like a tilled field in front of the temple. Meaty bones and scraps of bread lay trampled in the mud everywhere. The temple attendants silently carried the tables and benches away to the storehouse or scoured the inside of the temple before the feet of the indifferently staring gods.

She saw Holme through the thinning crowd. His face was drawn and tired; he had probably searched for her all night. He didn't ask her anything or get angry, just said they were ready to leave camp. He noticed a mark she had under one ear, a mark from two rows of strong teeth, but said nothing. Holme had feared he'd never see her again, that some chieftain had left with her, and deep in his sullen heart he was relieved.

On the way back, they heard a yell from a large group breaking camp, and suddenly found themselves standing before the chieftain and people from the old settlement. There was a momentary silence while everyone stared in disbelief; then the chieftain turned red in the face and harshly ordered Holme and Ausi back to the settlement with them. They'd get what was coming to them there.

Holme was confused for a moment; then he whispered to Ausi to run to the smiths' camp. He'd follow soon. As she responded, she saw him pull out the knife he had under his clothes.

The chieftain hesitated before ordering Stor and Tan to take Ausi. With quick, frightened looks at Holme, they started running, but he rushed them with the knife, chasing them in a semicircle out toward the field.

People all around stopped what they were doing and watched the spectacle. Someone yelled that fighting was forbidden in the temple area. A band of riders on their way home galloped up.

Stor and Tan had stopped out in the field, and a little ways away stood Holme, knife in hand. He asked them scornfully why they didn't want to fight him. Was abandoning babies in the woods and catching women all they were good for? All the time, out of the corner of his eye, he was watching Ausi, who soon reached the smiths' camp.

The chieftain, seeing there might be trouble and unpleasantness, yelled irritably for the thralls to come back. The court had already sat, and he knew that he had no legal right to Holme. They had found him, a black-haired, angry boy, on an islet – a 'holme' –

and that had given him his name. But Ausi had been born at the settlement, so she definitely belonged to him. He was running short of thralls and would have been glad to have both of them home with him again. He had missed his skillful smith many a time.

The festival and the court were over, but maybe there was some other way to get the thralls back. You could never just talk with Holme; you had to do something else.

Stor and Tan returned like big, chastised dogs, and the warriors glared contemptuously at them. The chieftain ordered everyone to go on and break camp and forget Holme until later. Off in the distance a group of men came running from where Ausi had fled, doubtless to help Holme. A fight here would never do. Holme walked toward them, and they gathered in a menacing group a short distance away. The smiths held their long-handled axes close to their bodies so they wouldn't be noticed in the sacred area.

They stood there a moment, but the people from the settlement ignored them and kept working. Holme explained the situation in a few words to his friends, and they were all on his side. He was too good a man to be a thrall for the short-legged, broad-nosed pig of a chieftain they saw over there.

The smiths gradually retreated toward their camp, where the women were clustered in an anxious group watching them. The beer was gone, the food spoiled, and the older women knew that there was usually trouble on the way home. Many of the groups hauled silent bodies with them under the skins for many days so they could lie in peace in the earth of their fathers.

Seeing his former thralls had provoked the chieftain, and he plotted how he could get them back to the settlement. He sent Stor and Tan to see which way they had gone. Maybe he would get his chance if they were traveling in the same general direction.

The chieftain didn't want to attack them openly. He had seen the big smiths with their axes; it would be hard to overpower them. But he could follow them for a while; maybe they would split up farther down the road, leaving the thralls alone. Smiths traveling by foot couldn't walk very far the first day.

Ausi watched the temple and the huge mounds recede into the distance and disappear on the horizon. Their group trudged sullenly and silently all day, enjoying nothing. Wagons and bands of riders splashing along the muddy road passed them continually.

Though she missed her baby, Ausi recoiled at the thought of returning to town. Everything had seemed so bright and joyous while the stranger was there; now, since he had brought light and then disappeared, it was even darker than before. But he had said there is no death, so maybe he'd return. She'd have to be there in that case so he could find her.

Holme had said nothing about her running away and performing every imaginable act with other men. She shouldn't have done that, but it was his and the beer's fault. And the singing and dancing! She didn't want to think about it anymore, but no wonder things had gone as they did. She would never think about doing those things with other men at home.

If they would only set up camp early now so she could sleep. None of them had slept more than a couple of hours at dawn for several days. And Ausi hadn't slept at all the last night. She must have taken a wrong turn since those were nobles she had ended up with in the temple. She remembered expensive clothes and gilded walls, soft beds. They might have thought she was some chieftain's daughter. A man had whispered the smiling god's name in her ear, saying she was his loyal servant. But she wasn't – she must have been mistaken for someone else.

The smiths and their women looked for their old campsite and stayed there again. The spruce twigs were dry and warm from the sun, and there was plenty of firewood. No one had to tend the fire; it could go out and they would be all right under the skin rugs the rest of the night.

Many people passed by, and some camped near them, but they didn't hear the laughing and yelling they had on the way there. After the smiths had eaten meat and old bread, they immediately lay down under the skins and slept heavily.

It wasn't completely dark yet when a noise awakened them. The softly burning fire shone on men standing around the camp. The smiths groped furiously for their axes, but they were gone.

The chieftain spoke calmly, saying he didn't want to harm them; he only wanted his due. They'd better give him Holme and Ausi. Then they could lie down to sleep again peacefully, and they'd get their weapons back.

Ausi's first anguished thought flew to her baby. What would happen to her if neither parent returned? They might carry her into the woods again if there was no one to answer for her.

The chieftain and the master smith exchanged a few words, but it was already clear what would happen. At least twelve armed warriors were surrounding five unarmed smiths. Holme was holding his knife, but what good would that do against several swords? He was ordered to give it up.

'You can have it when you come back,' the master smith said quietly to him, certain he wouldn't remain long in servitude. Everyone was watching him, the warriors vigilantly, Stor and Tan anxiously. Finally, Holme handed his knife to the master smith and gave himself up. The master smith asked the chieftain to treat Holme and his woman well but got no response.

The prisoners walked between Stor and Tan toward the large camp not far away. The chieftain's wife looked uneasily at Holme's dark face. In vain she had asked her husband not to bring the two thralls back. She also noticed with hatred that Ausi had grown even more beautiful since the last time she saw her. Surely the tranquillity now characterizing the settlement would vanish once Holme and Ausi returned.

No one tied up the prisoners, but two men at a time kept guard over them at night. Holme finally managed to ease Ausi's mind about the baby; she knew they'd take good care of her. The master smith was expecting them back soon, so he'd obviously protect the child.

Holme had already decided they'd go back to the settlement before trying to escape. He couldn't free himself and Ausi without weapons, but he'd soon have some once he got to his old smithy.

Stor and Tan looked extremely uncomfortable at the idea of having Holme back. He noticed that and smiled ominously at them. The chieftain and the warriors ignored the prisoners once they had them secured.

They broke camp early and traveled on miserable forest roads, where a few patches of snow still dotted the north sides of boulders. Toward evening of the second day, Holme began to recognize the area, and after a while, they could hear dogs barking from the settlement. The dogs had caught their distant scent and soon came bounding and barking merrily toward them in the forest. A couple of the dogs recognized Holme and almost ate him up. He smiled contentedly and patted their heads.

The road passed the smithy, and Holme looked in with curiosity. Everything was in disarray, and he snorted scornfully at the work that was lying in view.

Before the chieftain left them and went into the hall, he made a little speech. He said they deserved to be severely punished, but everyone was tired, and he would let it go if they would work faithfully and behave. If they tried to escape again, nothing could save them.

Holme listened to the threats with only half an ear, but Ausi was alarmed and cried about her baby, so far away. Holme was usually right, though, and he had told her several times during the trip that the baby would be taken care of until they could get back to town for her. She hoped the wait wouldn't be long.

Ausi got back her old place in the thralls' quarters. Her friends were endlessly curious about everything that had happened to her while she had been away. They told her that the oldest woman thrall had died and that her ashes lay under a barely visible mound above the fields. And the mighty Stenulf was no longer there; he had vanished just after they escaped.

The next day, both Holme and Ausi looked with malicious pleasure at the chieftain's child, who ran around with a rigid, forward-bent head. He was a big, spiteful child. His mother was always nearby, watching him with uneasy eyes. When the child caught sight of Holme, he stared at his face a moment, then ran screaming for his mother.

The concern for his own baby could not drive away Holme's satisfaction in being the master smith again. His helpers busied themselves officiously around him, anxious to please. Plows and spades stood outside awaiting repair for spring; kettles with broken handles, bent swords, and blunted spearheads were strewn everywhere. Most of the ax material was still where he had seen it last.

The chieftain listened contentedly to the new ringing in the sledgehammers' song. He had secretly posted guards during the night, but no one had tried to escape. He had used a couple of the least valuable thralls so the loss wouldn't be too great if Holme killed them. But the night had passed, and they were still alive and trembling when day broke.

The long ship lay on shore, almost finished. It was more beautiful than the old one, even though the dragon head was still bare wood. The chieftain and the warriors kept busy with the ship all day, and Holme had orders to produce some smithwork for it that his helpers couldn't do on their own.

Ausi wandered around, her heart heavy with longing for her baby, but at the same time she was a little proud of her clothes, which were much better than her companions'. She talked about the town, too, and their hut, and the treasures she had there. If it hadn't been for her baby, she would have gladly stayed at the settlement, at least for a little while. But as always, Holme would decide what was best for them. That night maybe she'd hear what he had figured out.

The new clearing was finished and had borne a year's worth of crops. The pigs were already out, skinny and dirty after the winter. They grubbed in the refuse heap and plowed long furrows in the ground with their snouts. There was still a layer of dry leaves and grass in the barn for the horses and cows.

The chieftain marked out a new patch of ground for the thralls to clear in their spare time. He was convinced that this year, the first after the abundant sacrifices, would be a rich one. That's how it had been the last time.

Ausi's first job was to help with the spring cleaning. The provisions shed and storerooms had to be swept and aired, the high hall and holy room scrubbed and decorated. The shrine had only one inhabitant, a war god, his crude wooden statue painted red and gold.

The second night, two warriors wandering the forest came home while there was still a little daylight. They headed toward the women thralls' building, wrangling over who'd get the one who had just come home. They talked about how much more appealing she was than other women in the settlement.

But a dark, motionless figure sat guard on a rock on the hillside. The warriors stopped outside the building when they caught sight of him, then hesitated, talking in low voices. They both knew who was sitting on the rock. They couldn't mistake the broad shoulders and head lowered like a wild animal ready to spring.

'Get out of here!' one of the warriors ordered in a harsh, muffled voice, but the figure neither answered nor moved.

The warriors thought a while longer. The silent figure outside made them lose their desire for the women. Besides, they might get a knife in the back when they turned to crawl in through the low door. It always annoyed them to have to bend over and crawl; it was demeaning and made them feel helpless.

The warriors withdrew from the thralls' dwelling in a rage and walked toward the high hall for bed. They would rather have cut the thrall down with a sword, but the chieftain wanted him there, and besides, there was no telling how the fight might end. The thrall was strong and wild and couldn't be scared off; there would have to be a fight.

The next day, Holme and Ausi agreed she would call for him if any warrior tried to pay her an evening visit. They both knew that none of the thralls would dare even look at her. Holme also told her that he would soon have weapons and equipment ready so they could leave. He had paid attention to the road and was confident he could find his way back to where they'd been ambushed.

They stood in the dusk a while, holding hands, talking about the baby and their hut. Deep down, Ausi felt like crying at the thought of the stranger's not being around anymore, of not being anywhere.

A thrall from another farmstead came panting through the woods a little after sunrise. His message caused the chieftain to assemble his warriors with an angry roar. His wife stood mute and ashen faced while the stiff-necked son bent back to see his father's face.

The thrall came from his father-in-law's farmstead, asking the chieftain for help. The farmstead was under attack from a hostile family, much greater in number than the defenders. No one had seen the thrall or known that he had run for help. He had taken off before sunup.

In a short time, the warriors were ready. The chieftain gave brief orders about the work and animals to those staying at home. He ordered Stor and Tan to come along, thought a moment, then gestured toward Holme. 'We'd better take you along,' he said. He didn't worry about Ausi; he knew she'd do nothing without Holme.

Holme hesitated only an instant. He knew if he refused, he'd be cut down before the warriors left. The chieftain was always on the brink of rage.

The chieftain didn't say good-bye to his wife and child, but he cast a strange, almost sorrowful look at them before rushing down to the ships at the head of the warriors.

The farmstead was located on the other side of a large cove, and they would save a lot of time by sailing across instead of running around it as the thrall had. Those staying at the settlement saw them hop into the old ship, and soon seven pairs of oars were slicing through the water. Farther out the wind picked up, and the black and yellow sail filled.

After they had disappeared beyond the point, the chieftain's wife ordered a year-old male calf to be slaughtered. She went to the shrine and anxiously studied the battle god's forbidding face. The thralls came soon with the frothing blood, and she ordered the oldest one to make the offering. As a woman, she didn't dare provoke the god by smearing him with the branch. He would doubtless rather have a man do that, even if it was a thrall.

Ausi walked into the high hall to put it back in order after the hurried departure. The warriors had sorted through their weapons and thrown the ones they didn't want on the floor. She was sure Holme would return before the others so they could get away with no one there to prevent them. What could women and thralls do against Holme?

In the middle of the day, the chieftain's wife sent a couple of thralls up to the lookout hill. When they came down, they said smoke was rising from her father's farmstead. Ausi watched the edge of the forest almost constantly and put in order what she could, but no one came. Still she did not grow anxious. Holme always knew best.

The forest on the north side of the besieged farmstead was dense, and the warriors could have gained a great advantage if they had circled around and attacked from there. But their pride urged them over the glade by the most direct route. Holme felt contemptuous, realizing how many they could have killed with arrows or spears before anyone even knew they were there.

A joyous cry from the besieged women and children greeted the new arrivals. Their assailants quickly retreated toward a large feed shed to protect their backs. A warrior lay to one side by a rock, holding his side and looking at the newcomers. The spear that had wounded him lay beside him. Several arrows were stuck in the timber wall.

The chieftain ordered the thralls to stay back during the attack. Stor and Tan hurried straight into the woods, and Holme sat down on a rock at the forest's edge. The enemy men at the feed shed were shooting arrows, but all their arrows were either deflected by shields or missed their marks. The men from the farmstead rushed out to join their allies.

Several men on both sides got spear wounds but none so serious they couldn't continue the battle. The women urged the wounded man by the rock to try crawling to them, but he shook his head. Gradually, one by one, the enemy was forced into the shed they were trying to keep at their backs. A couple of the enemy men stationed themselves in the doorway to cut down anyone trying to break in.

The shed was set off from the other buildings. The air was calm as the two chieftains conferred together and then gave one of their men an order. He sneaked behind the shed and struck his flint in the dry grass by the sun-warmed southern wall. He crammed it in under the logs and listened with glee as the leafy branches started crackling inside.

The men in the shed had no way of putting out the fire, which raged in the bed of dry branches left over from the year before. The men knew they'd backed into a trap, but they hadn't imagined their enemy would burn his own building.

They left their shields behind as they rushed out. The warriors outside, not expecting them so quickly, stood with shields in hand. Confusion spread among them, and a couple of them fell before the blows of the onrushing men.

Holme saw a big, raging group of men, swords flashing. His chieftain charged like an angry wild boar, and more than one man gave way before him. One of the enemies, unable to hold his ground against him, dashed away, picked up a spear, and flung it at the chieftain even though they should have been using only swords then. It hit him, lodging under one arm. The chieftain reeled, and another man hacked him with a sword as he fell.

The spear came out when the chieftain got up again. His face was white above his beard, and with wild, unseeing eyes, he rushed straight into the battle. He swung his sword wildly, and both friend and foe had to duck. He fell again closer to the fire, crawled a short distance, then collapsed. Holme watched him tensely, thinking that it would be a simple matter for him and Ausi to leave now whenever they pleased.

The heat forced the warriors back, and Holme had to move to another rock. The battle became less fierce after the chieftain fell, and then suddenly the enemy chieftain called loudly for a truce. His warriors gathered around him while the defenders placed themselves between the enemy and the farmstead. Holme alone saw the fallen chieftain suddenly kick his short legs out and then lie still. He could barely see Stor and Tan in the woods.

After the feed in the shed had burned, the fire continued to lick the charred walls a while but then weakened and sank toward the ground. When the battle was over, the women and thralls from the farmstead came and threw water on the hissing timber. The burned feed lay inside the shed, a smoldering black mass.

The warrior by the rock had bled to death; the chieftain and three other fallen warriors had stopped moving too. Many others had bloody faces and arms. A young woman came from the hall and sat silently beside one of the dead.

The rock Holme was sitting on was cold, so he moved to some sun-warmed moss. He was almost indifferent about the outcome of the battle now that the chieftain was gone. A woman ruled him and Ausi now, and that practically meant they could go wherever they wanted. Even the warriors might not stay at the settlement but instead find another chieftain or go home to their relatives' farmsteads.

He saw the two bands of warriors reach an agreement. The outsiders lifted their dead on their shoulders and walked down toward the lake while a dismal group of warriors surrounded the chieftain's body. He had buried his face in a layer of moldering leaves on the ground. In the sunshine by one of the other fallen warriors, a woman sat as motionless as the warrior.

Stor and Tan approached from the woods. As they stood by the chieftain's body, they feigned dismay, but Holme knew they had trouble hiding their glee. They'd have even more power now that just a woman ruled over them.

The woman's father, the old chieftain of the farmstead, ordered the thralls back to work. But he asked the thrall who had run for help independently to step up and made him foreman over the others. The thrall received new clothes from the storehouse and walked out beaming to abuse his underlings.

The warriors carried their dead chieftain to the ship, then returned to the farmstead to eat and drink. Down by the door Holme could hear them talking about what would happen now. The old chieftain could take his daughter and her child home with him until the boy grew up and was able to take over the settlement. The thralls could stay and tend to everything the same as before. He'd send someone to keep an eye on them if none of the warriors stayed on as overseer.

But no one responded; the warriors had wanted adventure for many a summer and had no desire to tie themselves to a farmstead. They thought silently of the dragon ship that would soon be ready. No one had more right to it than they did. What would a woman do with a warship? The old boat would still be good enough for the fishing grounds.

There was no cry of rage or promise of revenge for the chieftain: his in-laws had nothing to say about him, good or bad; Holme, Stor, and Tan felt relieved and thought of the advantages his death would bring; the warriors seemed a little more enthusiastic, glad their lives were about to move into a new phase.

The chieftain's wife had been standing in the yard of the settlement almost all day. The thrall who periodically descended the hill had reported that the smoke had thinned out and disappeared just before noon. The work was almost done; earlier the crops had been sown, and the chieftain himself had participated. Arms swinging and a bushel basket hanging from his waist, the stocky figure had walked up and down the fields the last two days. On the hillside above the fields was a little stone altar where he offered sacrifices to the harvest god before and after the sowing.

A dog at the forest's edge suddenly started howling protractedly, and a shudder ran through the whole settlement. It must mean one of their warriors had fallen, one or many. From way below the hill, they could see the thrall shaking his head as the howling reached him. After a moment, he came running down and said he could see the ship in the distance. The wind had settled toward evening, so the sail wasn't up.

Ausi wasn't anxious about Holme despite the dog's howling. She knew he wouldn't have been allowed to fight even if he had wanted to. But when the ship approached, she was standing right beside the chieftain's wife like her equal. Both had a husband on the ship. Both shielded their eyes with their hands when the ship moved into the dazzling sunlight and out of sight for a while.

Ausi had been more independent since her return, and the

chieftain's wife eyed her with distaste even in the midst of her apprehension. How dared she stand there in the courtyard waiting for the ship even if her thrall husband was on it?

As the ship approached, the thralls began moving again. No one knew what kind of mood the chieftain would be in or whether he was already watching them. A sow was farrowing in one part of the pigsty with a thrall watching over her. Whenever she tried to bite one of the squirming piglets, the thrall kicked her in the snout. He announced the arrival of each new piglet with a loud yell toward the hall. A sow that already had a litter ambled on the hillside, surrounded by piglets. From a distance she looked like a big rock capping a mound of little ones.

The chieftain's wife did not see the familiar squat figure step up on the gangway first, as he usually did. She saw the men tending to some heavy objects in the ship, and Ausi noticed her lips turn white and rigid. She looked around for her little boy and picked him up though he kicked and flailed his arms.

Ausi had seen Holme's black head already, and then he hopped ashore, followed by Stor and Tan. The thralls waded in the water and steadied the gangway for the warriors to walk over with their heavy loads.

With eyes wide, the chieftain's wife again searched the group of men, but they were all too tall. The chieftain had to be among the inert forms they had laid on the ground as they looked apprehensively toward the settlement. They picked them up now and started up the path. The chieftain's wife backed all the way to the wall to make way for them. Standing there with her little boy as they walked past with the dead, she listened to their heavy steps, but their eyes stared grimly ahead. Almost all of them had bloody faces and arms.

The little boy in her arms held still now, watching the warriors.

Ausi walked toward Holme, who had anchored the ship and was coming across the field toward the thralls' dwelling. Stor and Tan positioned themselves silently near their mistress to await orders.

Even though no one was guarding Holme and Ausi, they were no longer so eager to leave. Holme wanted to see what would happen to the settlement. Ausi was curious about how the chieftain's wife would handle everything, the funeral feast and building of the burial mound. Both felt a profound sense of well-being in knowing the chieftain was gone forever. Standing at the edge of the forest where the blue flowers were fading and losing their petals, they agreed to wait until all this was over. Holme assured her again that they would get their baby back safe and sound.

After the warriors had carried in the dead, there was complete silence. You could distinctly hear the seabirds screeching and the shouts from the pigsty whenever a new piglet arrived. The thrall watching over the sow hadn't realized anything was happening in the settlement. The other thralls stood, their eyes fixed on the chieftain's wife, waiting for something to happen.

The warriors saw the remains of the offering at the shrine and asked who had made it. They shook their heads at a thrall having wielded the bloody branch; now they knew why things had gone so badly. The battle god had been insulted. It would have been better if the chieftain had made time for the sacrifice before they went into battle.[22]

No one talked at all that night. The chieftain's wife took her place after leaving the child with a woman thrall. From the high hall, she heard the warriors clearing their throats and chewing their evening meal. She saw the god's image in the darkness of the shrine, and the smell of blood drifted out. The child and the old

22. See p. 86, note 14.

nurse lay in the bed she had shared with the chieftain.

A couple of moldering leaves had stuck in the chieftain's beard, and she plucked them out. His clothes were bloody and torn near his left shoulder. The warriors had put his sword with the ornate hilt on his chest. Through the window behind the god, she saw a couple of motionless treetops against the sky, which grew darker and darker.

Once she heard some mumbling outside; the pigsty door closed, and then all was quiet. A warrior snored heavily in the darkness. The chieftain's body gradually disappeared from view in the soft darkness and was invisible an eternity. His sword hilt was the first thing to catch the rays of the dawning sun.

The warriors started digging the grave the next morning. The chieftain would lie beside his father and grandfather in the grove of memorial stones. The thralls gathered fuel, a huge stack of dry wood, for the funeral pyre.

In the hall, the chieftain's wife prepared food for the dead man's journey. Some chickens were killed and cooked; a bronze pot was filled with soup.

The memorial stone was already in the grove, taken there by the chieftain himself before he died. The spades struck rock scarcely an arm's length into the earth, and everyone said it was deep enough.

At midday, two dragon ships from the relatives' farmstead sailed up to the jetty carrying the chieftain's father-in-law, brothers-in-law, and other relatives with women and children. Some sacrificial animals were also brought ashore – two goats the old chieftain wanted to sacrifice for the dead man's success on his journey.

The funeral pyre was ready and the chieftain's body was carried down to it. He had on everyday clothes but no weapons. Only his knife remained in his belt, its bronze sheath shining. A flint and some other little things were left in his pockets. Behind the warriors carrying the body, everyone walked single file, the noblest first and the thralls last. The wood in the pyre had been artfully stacked as in a charcoal mill, and there was a skin rug on top.

Before the father-in-law lit the funeral pyre, the chieftain's wife threw handfuls of blue and white flowers on the corpse as a gift to the gods. The flowers rained down over the chieftain, settling like stars everywhere, in his hair and beard, on the skin rug and the wood.

Powder-white smoke from the dry leaves poured out of the pyre after the father-in-law lit it. Smoke rose up and floated among the tops of the young aspens, which had begun sprouting tiny leaves and long, pendulous stems. The birds fell silent and flew off toward the forest.

The fire, crackling and popping, took hold in the wood, driving those standing closest to it away with its heat. It looked red and malicious in the sunshine. A gust of wind pushed it to one side, revealing for an instant the chieftain's ghastly head with the hair and beard burnt off.

The heat intensified, and the fire crept into the half-dry grass. Thralls stood with their spades, ready to throw dirt on the fire. They called to each other under their breath and laughed when no one was looking. It was a good day for them – a real change and some light work.

The flames reached higher yet, and there was something festive in their roar. The warriors watched with approval, thinking it was a good sign for the chieftain. The child laughed at the fire consuming his father, but the mother stared into it with a rigid face.

Ausi and Holme dared stand next to each other and watch the

funeral pyre. They felt relieved and happy; they could go wherever and whenever they wanted. And the man they hated above all others, the one who had despised them and had condemned their baby to death, who had brought them back into slavery, lay burning on the pyre in front of them. There he was now; he could never do anything to them again.

Ausi watched the smoke, wondering when the chieftain would continue his journey to the realm of the dead. Sometimes she imagined she saw his bearded face high up among the white-gray smoke billowing toward the blue sky.[23] The stranger had said that there was only one home after death, and that was with his god. The chieftain couldn't go there. It was difficult to understand it all, and now she had no one to ask.

An unexpected puff of wind drove the smoke among the onlookers, forcing them to one side. The smell was foul and was sometimes accompanied by a soft hissing sound. The child played by his grandfather's memorial stone, hiding behind it and peeking out. He turned his whole body in the direction he wanted to look.

Holme had long since tired of it all and wanted to be on his way – back to the smithy or the forest. But that would cause offense, and there was no need for any disturbance with everything turning out so well. He wanted to see what it would be like at the settlement now and just who was going to stay on to run things. It might be someone from the other farmstead.

23. In chapter 9 of the Old Norse *Ynglinga Saga*, the first part of the *Heimskringla*, Snorri Sturluson explains the importance of smoke at a funeral pyre: 'It was people's belief that the higher the smoke rose into the sky, the more elevated in heaven would he be who was cremated' (Snorri Sturluson, *Heimskringla: History of the Kings of Norway*, trans. Lee M. Hollander [Austin: Univ. of Texas Press, 1964], p. 13). See also line 3155 of the Old English poem *Beowulf*, where the poet describes the hero's funeral pyre and burial: 'Heaven swallowed the smoke.'

Holme had already made weapons and hidden them in a safe place. Ausi could get food for the journey, at least bread; there was enough meat to be had once they were under way. A few days' journey through the wilds would be enjoyable.

His thoughts returned to the chieftain on the pyre. That's how it should have been for Stenulf, too – Stenulf, who was a much bigger and better warrior than the chieftain. He had been lying under the mound on the ridge for three summers.

Maybe he was still there, unable to move on and without food for the journey. The stranger's god hadn't even helped his own follower; he couldn't raise up Stenulf either. Ausi believed the stranger would return, but she was a woman and believed all sorts of things.

The swineherd was busy at the sty, the only man not by the pyre. Some women, occasionally visible between the high wall and provisions shed, were preparing for the feast. The sacrificial goats gnawed on the tender grass, looked toward the lake, and bleated. After the pyre had burned and the mound had been raised, they'd be sacrificed to the gods.

The roasted birds and bronze pot were a little ways from the fire. Holme figured the food would only last a couple of days for someone who ate as much as the chieftain did. But he might be able to find something on the journey if he had to.

The pyre would soon burn out; the smoke no longer billowed as before, but was hot and blue. The child had fallen asleep by the memorial stone; the woman thrall sat next to him keeping watch. Everyone knew the grove was full of snakes; they lived in caves during the winters and would come out and sun themselves as soon as the ground was bare and the previous year's leaves were dry.

There were good-sized waves out on the cove, but the belt of reeds checked them so only tiny, glistening swells rolled in among the stones on shore. The warriors glanced frequently toward the new ship painted dark red with gold trimming on the prow and stern. On the shore lay some leftover oak that the chieftain had intended for a fishing boat to replace the one Holme had stolen.

After the flames had died down, the black mass of ashes that had once been the chieftain was still hissing slowly. His father-in-law took a spade and pushed aside most of the cinders; some metal objects glistened in the ashes. The thralls were ordered to throw water on the smoldering ground so he could walk closer to the pyre.

When it had cooled off a little more, he took the ash urn, an ornamented clay pot, and began scooping the yellow-gray ashes, remains of the chieftain's flesh, into it. The fire hadn't touched the bones; they were still intact, smoking from the heat. The father-in-law piled them beside himself and continued scraping up the ashes. A clasp or some iron fittings sparkled now and then in the heap of ashes. The chieftain's wife, her face pale, looked on.

When he finished, the old chieftain washed the bones and laid them beside the urn. Finally he laid down the provisions for the journey. The people standing closest to him handed him rocks to stack around the burial objects to protect them. He covered the urn with a flat stone. Then he got up, and numerous spades started throwing dirt back into the grave.[24]

When it was level with the ground, he said they would leave it that way until later. They'd finish after they had eaten, then raise the memorial stone, and finally offer sacrifices to the battle god for the chieftain's good reception.

24. Except for the wife's throwing flowers on the corpse, the details of the burial scene are based on archeological evidence. See Schön, *Fridegård och forntiden*, p. 116.

Most of them found it hard to hide their pleasure at the thought of leaving the hot burial grove, getting washed, and sitting down to eat. No one missed the chieftain except his wife; his death had created new vistas for the others and brought relief to their lives.

By the time night fell, three memorial stones stood an equal distance from each other in the grove. They were visible from the settlement now, but the foliage would soon grow dense and hide them for some months. The new mound would be bare the first year; in the second summer, sparse blades of grass would creep over it, and after four years, it would be just like the other two. A thousand years later, one of the stones would fall down, but the other two would still be standing, and the mounds would remain unchanged. By then the shore would have receded a good distance from the grove.

The old chieftain decided how the settlement would be managed after he left and took his daughter with him. The thralls would take care of everything by themselves until he designated someone to come and take command.

He called the people together and determined which jobs and duties they had had up until then. Stor and Tan stood by watching smugly; they were sure they'd be named foremen since they were so conscientious. Holme stood farthest away, watching it all indifferently, but he noticed the old man's eyes searching him out. The chieftain had seen many weapons and tools made by Holme's hand and even carried a sword of Holme's making fastened to an expensive foreign hilt. He realized the thrall was stubborn and dangerous, but then he probably had to be because of the chieftain they had just burned. The escape and recapture had been related to him, and he realized no one could keep the smith and his woman there now against their will. The chieftain was old and wise, and in most matters, his vision was clear.

'You'll be in charge here,' he said amicably to Holme. 'You know how everything should be. I'll come back now and then and see how it's going.'

Stor and Tan cleared their throats in surprise and disappointment, but the chieftain didn't pay any attention to them. Holme smiled self-confidently and straightened up when he was convinced the chieftain was serious. Yes, he could do that as well as anybody. The dead chieftain's wife started to object, but her father silenced her.

The warriors lost all interest in the settlement and absorbed themselves in the ship. In a few days it would be ready. No one denied their right to take the vessel they had built with their own hands. The old chieftain had asked if any of them wanted to stay on and take over the settlement and his daughter, but all remained silent. They had been waiting for too long for a chance to sail to distant lands.

After making his request, the chieftain boarded ship with his daughter, her child, and all his household servants. Ausi looked at Holme proudly and happily; they were like rulers now. She could repay her companions for all the harm they had done her.

That night, they sat alone in the large, empty hall, talking about retrieving their baby. Holme would return alone in a few days; he didn't think the thralls would dare do anything to Ausi while he was away. He could be back in three days if he went by horse.

They considered sleeping on the chieftain's bed, but went to the thralls' dwelling instead. There was no need to provoke the warriors, who would be leaving soon anyway. The women thralls had just come in and were setting the long table with the warriors' meal so it would be there when they returned from the lake.

In the thralls' dwelling, friends were talking, both men and women, in sullen, threatening tones about the new situation. They'd gladly work for the chieftain's wife or some new chieftain, but Holme and Ausi weren't as dependable as they were and shouldn't try lording it over them.

The battle god stood mute and forgotten in his shrine. The old chieftain had ordered a sacrifice out on the field, but he hadn't said anything about the god inside. A farmstead without warriors was in no need of his favor.

A warm wind was blowing across the hillsides the day the warriors sailed away. They hauled ample supplies down to the ship, whole chests of bread and meat. Holme had examined their weapons and given them new arrows.

The long glistening red grass surged around them as they walked down to the shore around midday. The freshly gilded dragon gaped toward the cove, its spiky red tail turned toward land.

The thralls stood in a group at the settlement, watching the warriors sail away. After they had passed the point, the sail fluttered out, filled, then stretched toward the open sea. The dragon picked up speed and ducked behind the point, its length glistening as the oars were pulled in. The next instant, it was gone.

The thralls sat down where they were, not knowing what to do. It felt strange, almost unsettling, not to have to fear the chieftain's hard eyes. Holme was nowhere to be seen; naturally he was thinking about leaving and he wasn't their master anyway.

A rhythmic shuffling noise came from the provisions shed. Ausi and Holme were amusing themselves by grinding with the new hand mill the chieftain had gotten while they were away. It consisted of two round, notched stones; the upper one was pulled around with a heavy stake set in a hole. You could mill many times faster with it than by rolling a stone in a worn groove to crush the grain. The old millstone lay discarded on the hillside now, and when rain fell, sun-warmed water stayed in it for many days for the birds to bathe in and the dogs to lap noisily.

When Holme left, the seed the chieftain had sown had already sprouted, lightly covering the gray field. Nettles and oily grass were growing high up the pigsty wall. He had told the other thralls what to do while he was away, and they had answered either with scornful grins or silence. But he knew the most important things would get done anyway. He had also told them that if anyone touched Ausi, he wouldn't live to see the sun set in the forest the day Holme returned.

Holme had fixed up some old riding gear and had made a new bridle to go with it. He wasn't accustomed to riding and so he walked long distances, leading the horse by the reins. He followed along the ridge by the cave and saw Stenulf's burial mound again. The top stone had fallen down, but he would put it up again on the way back. The footpath between the cave and the spring was no longer visible. He longed for the days he had lived with Ausi in the cave.

His ax hung by a loop on the saddle so he could grab the handle. People he ran into looked with surprise at the powerful, melancholy figure on the little shaggy horse. His broad cheekbones and black locks of hair made him look like a wooden god.

By the next morning, he could recognize where they had been ambushed by the warriors. There were still some dry twigs and soot left from the camp. The chieftain hadn't derived much joy from what he had done that day.

Riding became easier and easier, and night was still hours away when he passed through the last forest and came to the shore.

There was the wide, blue lake, there the market town with its swarms of ships, people, and animals.

Holme left his horse at a farmstead near the ferry. In the boat, he enjoyed the thought of how surprised the smiths would be when he came striding into the smithy. 'I'm back for my knife,' he'd quip to the master smith. Then they'd hear how well things were going for him and Ausi now.

On shore, he walked straight to where Ausi had left the child before they had gone to the festival. The hut was on the outskirts of town, and a middle-aged woman had been well paid for caring for the child during those nine days.

In a garbage pile near the outskirts, a couple of dogs were scrounging for something to eat. Holme, looking indifferently at them, noticed something moving in the trash. He discerned a tiny black head and a pair of skinny arms and hands digging in the garbage and occasionally putting something in its mouth. With a roar, he rushed up the slope, and the dogs dashed away, snarling.

The child's hair was a single twisted knot of dirt, and she was holding a crust of bread in her hand when he picked her up. At first she just chewed listlessly, her dark eyes staring at him; then she began trembling and screaming with joy as she reached for her father's face. She had a little skirt on, but her arms and legs were bare, dirty, and scratched.

For the first time he could remember, Holme felt tears running down his cheeks. But his rage exploded at the same time, and, still weeping, he raced down the garbage heap toward the hut, the child under his left arm, his ax in his right hand. A couple of women who had seen it all ran after him at a distance to see what would happen.

The woman responsible for the child was standing in the doorway. She saw him coming, the child under his arm and the ax in his hand, and she ran screaming from the hut to seek protection. She ran toward the fortress, looking frantically around, screaming with fear. Holme pursued her silently and swiftly. Terrified faces peered out from everywhere, and a warrior coming out of a side street stopped and watched them.

They were still a good distance from the fortress when Holme caught up with the woman, whose legs were almost paralyzed with fear. Without breaking stride, he hit the back of her neck with the flat of his ax. She tumbled on her face, and he kept running toward the lake.

The oarsman said nothing about Holme's haste or his strange cargo; instead he quickly began rowing. Soon several men and women appeared at the shore, screaming and pointing at the boat. Holme glared grimly at the oarsman, who pulled even harder. His passenger's face made it clear that the oarsman's own life wouldn't be worth much if he tried turning around. He was an old man and no match for this black-haired man who looked as if he was made of granite.

Out in the middle of the cove, Holme realized he hadn't even had time to visit the smiths. Everything had happened faster than he would have wished. He couldn't turn back. He didn't regret teaching the woman a lesson, but it was good that she only got the flat of his ax. He could sense the blow hadn't been fatal, but she'd certainly have a headache. Maybe the smiths would hear about his visit and figure out what happened. They could have kept an eye on the child, though.

A long ship set out from the market town, and the oarsman gestured at it as he tried to row faster. It had to be the town guard after them. The child clung to Holme, never taking her eyes off him.

Before he jumped ashore, Holme clipped off a piece of silver rod twice as long as the oarsman should have received. The other boat was still a good ways out but approaching rapidly. The horse, still in riding gear, was grazing outside the farmstead. The forest was just behind them so they could surely get away.

Holme looked around at the farmstead and could see he still had a little time. He ran into the house and asked for milk for the child; the woman brought a pitcher immediately. As the child drank greedily, the woman watched, feeling great pity for her.

The long ship touched bottom just as Holme disappeared into the woods, and the little horse scurried like a rat into the brush, its bridle dangling. Holme knew it would find its way better than he could. He had reshod it, so it climbed the rocky slopes like a cat.

He heard the shouting as his pursuers reached the farmstead, but soon everything grew quiet in the sun-warmed forest. After he had passed through the trees and the plain beyond, he stopped at the edge of the next forest. The horse began grazing immediately, and Holme sat down with his child. He tried to put her in the grass beside him, but she resisted, refusing to leave his arms. He gave her some soft bread and meat, which she ate voraciously.

For a few hours that night, she slept lying on his clothes, as he sat half-naked beside her. When daylight broke, he rode on, the child sleeping against his chest. As the day grew hotter, she drank springwater from her father's large, dark hand and ate the last of his provisions.

Holme rode past Stenulf's mound in the middle of the night, his left arm numb from the child's weight. Even then, a night mist hovered over the marsh far below, and somewhere a bird called. On the other side of the ridge, he could hear squeals from the wild boars mating and fighting in the dark, ancient forest.

The settlement was quiet, but the horse under him whinnied wildly when it smelled home. The child woke up and clasped her father tighter. He got off and released the horse, which trotted off at once to find its companions in the pasture. Someone bolted toward him from the women thralls' quarters, snatched up the child in the darkness, and examined her with tear-filled eyes.

Holme later tersely described the journey, and when he told Ausi about the woman he had hit with the ax, she reached out and caressed his cheek for the first time in a long while. The child was soon sleeping in her mother's arms, and they walked to the chieftain's quarters inside the high hall. It was empty and quiet inside; a couple of bows left behind by the warriors still hung on the wall. Ausi glanced furtively at the shrine where the figure of the god was standing in the darkness, silent and grim. What would he think of thralls occupying the chieftain's bed and so close to him?

The chieftain's wife had taken the best skins with her, but those she had left made a bed good enough for the thralls. Outside the skins, the dirt floor was cold and hard. They talked softly until the gray light shone through the hole in the roof and the song-thrush in the aspen grove sang its morning song. The sun was soon shining on the west edge of the light hole, and a bird's shadow occasionally flickered by. Around midday, when the door was open, swallows would rapidly fly in, make a pass through the swarm of mosquitos under the ceiling, and disappear through the hole. Sparrows fluttered in frequently, sitting on the wooden pegs in the wall, or hopping about on the clay floor.

Before anyone else awakened, Ausi was already up putting out a pot of water for the sun to warm. It wouldn't be easy to get the child clean. She thought with satisfaction about Holme's clubbing the woman with the ax. She must have just kicked the child out to fend for herself. What if Holme hadn't shown up?

When Ausi got up she felt dizzy and sick and realized she'd felt this way for some time now. She'd better ask for a potion from the old thrall woman who knew about medicinal herbs.

Three summers had passed since the child was born and they had lived in the cave. Everything had gone well for them, and now they had their child back. There were a few pieces of cloth in a chest; she finally dared take one to make clothes for her child.

But when day came and she asked the old woman for some medicine, she got a scornful laugh in reply. The woman turned her back on her and said that the evil would probably pass toward autumn time.

'Don't you understand?' she asked, turning around and pointing at the child Ausi was washing. A foreboding gloom descended on Ausi, and she thought immediately about the festival of sacrifice. She had wondered many times why she had acted as she did and was ashamed that she hadn't behaved as she should have. What would Holme say? He couldn't say anything until the child was born and he could take a look at it. But something inside told her it wasn't Holme's.

The black-haired youngster was soon clean, and she ran around in the sun, laughing, her hair still wet. When Stor and Tan walked by, Ausi couldn't resist asking them if they had noticed that the baby had made it home from the woods. Hadn't they done their duty three summers ago? The thralls didn't respond but looked with surprise at the child they had abandoned by a rock that summer night so long ago. Now it was running around here, perhaps destined for something special since it had been permitted to live.

Within a few days, the trees had come into leaf, hiding the three mounds – two green and one dirt gray – in the aspen grove. The thralls had only begun to realize fully that the feared and hated chieftain was gone, that they never again would have to hide from his fits of rage. Holme wasn't as bad an overseer as they had feared; he stayed in the smithy most of the time and let them take care of the fields and meadows as they pleased. He fixed the warrior's discarded weapons and didn't say anything if one of his fellows went off to the woods with bow and arrow.

The old chieftain showed up now and then and was invariably satisfied with what had been accomplished. The grain looked splendid, and the store of weapons and tools in the smithy grew. He never mentioned anything about sending a new chieftain to the settlement.

Each time, the old chieftain offered a sacrifice on the altar by the fields, but he entered the shrine only once. The battle god stood there; woodworms had eaten tiny round holes in his head, dropping wood particles onto his shoulders. The smell of blood had almost completely disappeared on the warm wind wafting in and out through the constantly open light openings.

The north wind played with the hair of the woman sitting on the rock as she contemplated her fallen chieftain and husband. It was a hard and bitter memory he had left behind, but he was still her husband. Her son played beside her, looking like a bull calf because of his stiff neck.

Soon the wind rustled the leaves in the aspen grove, making sun and shadow dance and twinkle on the three burial mounds, two green, one gray. Many hours later, the sun reached a flotilla of dragon ships. The settlement's warriors had recently joined it with their new ship and were happily following a powerful chieftain to distant lands for war. The chieftain's ship was the biggest they had ever seen; a full-grown man could sit in the dragon's red maw.

The rumor soon reached the warriors that this flotilla would join another even larger one farther away; they were astonished. Their big new ship was looking small and shabby, but they still felt fortunate to be part of the large fleet.

And so the summer, warm and calm, passed by in the settlement. Holme exercised his power only in the smithy and turned everything else over to Stor and Tan, who contentedly strolled through the meadows or fished in the cove. In the evenings they would stand and count the pigs and other small animals as they came in, just as the chieftain used to do. The responsibility did the thralls good, and the settlement was run as well as ever before.

When the grazing was good in the forest, the cows didn't come home for the milking, so the thrall women with their wooden pails had to search for them. They walked mostly through a large, dried-out bog where white and pink orchids rose candlelike from the grass as far as they could see. The sun was always low at milking time, so the bog soil was cold both morning and night. Dwarf pine trees grew on the grassy tufts, and brown birds of prey thrived there.

Sometimes the herd of cows came running toward the settlement at a wild, snorting gallop, and surrounded the outlying buildings with anxious bellowing. Stor and Tan would count them quickly and frequently would find an animal missing. Then they knew that a bear stood in the bog somewhere, eating and peering around with small, fierce eyes. Once the bear followed the herd all the way to the settlement; heavy and ponderous, it lumbered into the courtyard but retreated soon from the blaring horns, the shrieks, and the spears that spit up dirt all around it.

Ausi had begun to show signs of pregnancy. Her walk got heavier and her hair lost its luster. Occasionally she met Holme's eye and saw a question there, but she said nothing. It was best to wait and see. She didn't dare hope that the child would be dark-complectioned and black-haired like Holme. The thought of that drunken, lascivious night among the pine trees when she had trembled between a large, hot body and the ground was too firmly embedded in her memory. The child was from that night. She sensed it; she knew it.

With the warriors gone, the thralls began living in couples. Two older women were left alone, but they had tired of men long ago. Several couples moved into the high hall and made themselves at home. Ausi watched disapprovingly, but Holme let them be. After all, they themselves were living in the chieftain's quarters. When the old chieftain came, he didn't care where the thralls were living. He saw that the fields were tended and the animals cared for, and he was content. It seemed obvious to the old chieftain that all this was a result of his sacrifices to the god of harvest, and he continued to bring offerings every time he visited.

In a few years, his stiff-necked grandson could take over the settlement himself, with his mother's help. With that in mind, he encouraged the thralls to take good care of their children and to bear many. Quite a few of them were growing old and would no longer be alive when the new chieftain grew up and needed thralls for his settlement.

One day during the leaf harvest, Holme walked to the cave. A couple of years' worth of spruce needles had fallen on the rock by the door, indicating no one had been there. There was a hollow in the ground by the narrow opening; a badger had probably thought about settling in the cave. But the stony ground had been too hard to dig in, or perhaps it still held the scent of human beings and had scared him away.

The grass was still lying there, but the needles fell off the spruce branch when he touched it. He lay down for a while and thought. Deep inside he longed to live in the cave again, to stay in it forever. Of course, things were going well now – he was living like a chieftain. But sometimes he wanted to walk into the heart of the forest where there wasn't a single soul. There were men who lived in caves or small dens of earth and stone – fugitives and outlaws with long hair and beards, resembling wolves in their animal skins. He had always felt drawn to them.

But Holme had come to replace the stone on Stenulf's mound. Stenulf had been a mighty warrior and should have had a chieftain's funeral. If the stranger's god had been good for anything, he would have called Stenulf up from the dead, but as it was, he couldn't even save his own priest. The stranger was hanging in the sacrificial grove; by now the flesh of both animals and humans had probably rotted off the bones.

Holme plucked away the small stones so he could anchor the top slab better. It wouldn't fall over for many lifetimes now. As far as he could see into the future, whoever walked by would see that Stenulf was lying there.

But after he fixed the mound, Holme still wanted to stay a while; it was so isolated and pleasant on the distant gravel ridge. Down in the hollow, a few of the tall, long-legged birds were walking, looking very much like sheep from a distance. Once when an old thrall had tried to catch one, they had attacked and almost killed him.

Plenty of good grass was growing between the cave and the ridge, and for a moment Holme thought about bringing the others from the settlement to retrieve it. But he changed his mind at once; someone might discover the cave. He wanted to be the only one who knew about it; he never knew when he might need it again. Ships might come sailing into the cove some day carrying warriors from across the lake. Then he'd only have to drop everything and flee as fast as possible, now that there was no defense. Such things had happened in other places.

He'd visit the cave again one day and hide a few essentials – an ax and a spear, a bar of gold. He had one such bar from the town but had no use for it right now. At the settlement, you had everything you needed without having to pay for it the way you did out in the world.

From the ridge, he could see far out over the forests, fading into blue in the distance. Smoke was rising here and there. The dark fir forest was broken by an intermittent patch of deciduous trees, especially where the land sank toward a river or lake.

He walked home across the hollow, keeping an eye on the large birds, which had flocked together watching him as he passed. It would be strange indeed if he couldn't break the necks of a few birds if they attacked him.

The smaller birds that fluttered around your head chirping during the spring now sat silently among the tufts, only reluctantly getting out of the way. Their nests were doubtless nearby. Maybe this was where the women usually came to gather eggs.

As everyone expected, it was a good year after the great sacrifice. Grain and grass grew thick and tall, the animals retained their beauty and had numerous offspring. Many women who hadn't had children by their husbands for many years felt the results of the tribute they had brought to the fertility god in the spring nights during the festival of sacrifice. At many farmsteads, a field was consecrated to him, and the god got his allotted share of all that was born and grown.

The thralls finished their work in good time and had a few free days between harvesting the hay and then the grain. Nothing had happened during the whole summer even though from the lookout hill they had seen several flotillas of dragon ships sailing south. The chieftains doubtless wanted to test their luck in battle, which ought to be good after the great sacrifice. A wanderer told them that a vast flotilla of dragons was on its way west to conquer lands and property. Warriors from all over the north had joined it.

All during the late summer, Holme worked on a little boat he was making from the leftover oak wood from the long ship. The old ship was too big to fish with, and besides, a little boat might come in handy. No one knew how long the halcyon days of peace would last.

Ausi's movements became heavier and heavier, and her features hardened. The anxiety gnawed constantly, but she hadn't responded to Holme's silent question. She realized more and more how closely the time coincided with those two insane nights. Around the midwinter sacrifice, the difficult hour would be at hand. She could see that Holme's figuring was the same.

If it only had come during the summer so she could go out into the forest when the moment approached. She could examine the child alone there, and if it looked like Holme, she could go home again with joy. If not, then at least she would be alone to decide what would be the best thing to do.

If only there were someone who could give her advice and help. The stranger was gone, but she couldn't have talked to him about this anyway. And his god probably wouldn't help her. But if the stranger had told the truth, then neither he nor his god could really die; they were there but couldn't be seen. Maybe she could go into the forest and tell them how difficult it was for her right now.

Maybe they would hear and understand. The stranger had usually held his hands together and looked upward when he talked with his god, and she could do the same.

The stranger had said that since they had had water poured on their heads that day they belonged to his god. Then he ought to help her now, too. If she walked up on the lookout hill, then he would surely see her as long as he wasn't too far away.

Holme saw Ausi gathering pieces of cloth together, tying them up and wrapping them in an animal skin, then taking them outside to hide. She would step timidly to one side whenever they met; she tried to hide her condition as much as possible.

A thin crust of snow covered the ground, but the lake was still open. The sheep and goats stayed out during the days, gnawing on the hard-frozen ground and bleating, their yellow eyes directed at the outlying buildings.

Toward evening, Holme saw Ausi standing in a corner, clutching the back of a bench and groaning. He decided to sleep in the hall with the others that night so she could be alone with the old thrall woman who knew a little about everything. He was glad the worst would soon be over. When the baby was gone and Ausi was healthy again, everything would get back to normal. Neither would talk about it, and no one else would ever know what had happened at the festival of sacrifice.

Actually, the fertility god should probably receive an offering so everything would go well. When the chieftain's wife was having her baby, the chieftain stayed by the altar in the field the whole day. But why should thralls make offerings? They usually bore their children just as well without sacrifices, and it would probably be no different this time.

Out in the high hall, the thralls had built a fire, and it flickered on the wall in the chieftain's quarters. Holme realized he hadn't seen Ausi for a long time. She wasn't usually still outside at this hour, and she hadn't wanted to be with the others for some time.

He went outside and looked into the thralls' dwelling, but it was quiet and deserted. They had all moved in for the winter. The hillside was white with downy snow, but the sky was dark with a heavy vault of clouds. Where could Ausi have gone?

Suddenly remembering the bundle she had hidden, he checked its hiding place; it was gone. He went in and asked around in the high hall, but no one had seen her.

'You've probably driven her out in the woods,' said the old woman thrall scornfully. But what did she know? Stor and Tan laughed. All the men were fixing shoes or carving bowls and spoons. The women were busy with flax or wool. The meat was cooking and filling the entire hall with its fragrance, but Holme's anxiety drove him back out again.

If there had been a little more snow, Holme would have been able to see Ausi's footprints. She had to have gone to the woods, and he thought of the wolves and wild boars. He hurried along, his eyes glued to the ground in the fading light.

Where a trickle of water had run down the hillside from the stables, Holme caught sight of a track. The water hadn't frozen so hard that her foot couldn't break through it. At least he knew which way she had gone.

In the woods, he followed his instinct more than tracks. He found another sign by the shore of the marsh – a footprint again, filled with water and black against the snow. Farther out she had taken a wrong step, and both feet had gone through. She must be wet and cold.

Holme was soon across the marsh without sinking once, whereas Ausi had slogged for long stretches through the mire. He paused on the hillside and listened. He heard a strange shriek, but it wasn't a wolf or a great horned owl. He had never heard it before. It stopped, and he hurried on. He thought about Stenulf and and a shudder passed through him, but he had to pass by the mound.

Just below it, the howling started again. Fear ravaged him fiercely for a moment, but then he understood. Could a human being sound like that? He made no move forward but instead stood behind a boulder until the shrieking abated and then stopped once again.

Holme wondered how Ausi had managed to budge the stone from the cave opening. Once a long time ago she had tried but couldn't. It was a good thing there were still twigs and moss inside.

When there was a long silence, Holme sneaked up to peek through the opening. To his surprise, he saw a light inside. Ausi was just sitting up then, lighting a piece of wood with the one just burning out, and then wedging it in the air vent. It crackled, flickered, and shone on her as she lay back down again. Soon the screams started again, and he moved a short distance away so he wouldn't have to hear them so distinctly.

This time it was worse, and he paced around anxiously, wondering what he could do. For one fleeting moment, he thought it served her right; that's what she got for the festival of sacrifice.

When it grew quiet, Holme sneaked closer again and saw that Ausi was sitting up. He heard a strange sound and saw her take the stick from the wall and shine it on something in front of her. He sensed disappointment and despair in her swollen face as she put the stick back and began busying herself with the thing in her lap.

Holme waited a long time before he went in. Ausi screamed when she saw his black-haired head in the opening, but when she realized it wasn't a wolf or a bear, she threw a skin rug over everything before her. Then, filled with agony, her eyes probed his face. He noticed with surprise that she had carried a pot of warm water with her through the woods.

'Give it to me,' he said.

'You won't have to look at him; I can keep him out in the hut, you know. . . .'

'Give it to me!'

Sobbing, she lifted the skin and brought out the baby, who was screaming through a contorted red face. Long fair hair clung to his head. Ausi wrapped all her pieces of cloth around him and wanted to wrap him in the skin, but Holme stopped her. No sense wasting a good skin out in the woods. It was better for the baby without it, too.

Ausi wouldn't hand Holme the baby but laid it beside her instead; the baby looked like a big bundle of cloth. Holme took it and crept backward out through the opening. Ausi heard the faint cries die away, then stop.

Holme was glad all had gone well. It was unpleasant and almost beneath him to carry the child out, but who else would do it? No one else must know anything about this. He didn't care what the thralls thought. Ausi was herself again, and everything would soon be back to normal between them. Her beauty would return, and her hands, which had pushed him away for so long, would pull him to her once more.

Holme didn't have to walk far. Beyond the glade bright with snow, the forest was so dense that he couldn't see the trunks until he was on top of them. He left the baby beside a tree. When he reached the middle of the glade again, he listened, but all was quiet.

Ausi had stopped sobbing and asked Holme to wait outside until she said he could come in. He had to wait until she had the strength to walk; she didn't dare be alone. He responded gently to her and began pacing back and forth outside the cave. A couple of times, he heard her change the lighted stick. She must have brought a whole bundle of them with her. No wonder she had sunk in the marsh with so much to carry.

When he finally got to come in, she showed him where to sit. If he would wait while she rested a moment, they could go home. Neither mentioned the baby; Ausi thought about him with anguish but it was mingled with a strange hostility because of his fair hair. She had hoped to the last it would be Holme's baby even though she had a gut feeling it was not.

The night outside seemed endless; new stars came and went in front of the cave opening, and the silence was complete. The sticks were all gone, and they missed the light and mild warmth. It got gradually lighter, but it wasn't the sun coming. Far beyond the mound hung an oblong moon, which had risen after midnight and had slowly climbed above the black forest.

Holme would rather be home before anyone awakened, but he said nothing to Ausi. She sensed what he was thinking and suggested that they leave. Her feet were getting stiff from the swamp water that had filled her shoes, and she needed to move. She too longed for home, fire, meat, and bread.

Holme's hard arms supported her the whole way, and this time the marsh held under her feet. A fox barked hoarsely, morosely. Toward the end of their journey, the forest started smelling of morning, but they would still probably make it home before anyone could see them and figure out what had happened.

Already Ausi thought less despairingly about the baby left in the woods. It had surely already died, without having suffered too much. Ausi had accepted long ago that it wouldn't be allowed to live, so now she felt as though something important had finally been settled. She would never drink beer and watch the priests of fornication again. In fact, she'd gladly stay home next time there was a festival of sacrifice.

Everyone was asleep when they walked through the high hall. Holme built a fire at the far end of the fire pit where the ashes were still hot and some embers were glowing.

But deep in the woods a tiny blue face shone rigidly and questioningly back at the moon, which gradually sank among the dense branches of the spruce trees. The baby's new mother – cold – had not taken long to lull it to sleep.

The old thrall woman who knew about medicine lit into Holme the next day. How dared he put that baby out when the old chieftain had said the babies should live to be thralls for his grandson? She'd tell him about this the next time he came.

The old woman pursued Holme, scolding him, even though Ausi stuck her head out and defended him; she said it was her own and Holme's business what they did with their baby. Not until Holme bent down for a stone did the old woman turn and run into the hall, dogs leaping around her excitedly.

Holme took her threats calmly. All he had to do was tell the chieftain that the baby was from the festival of sacrifice, and he'd understand. Not many of the babies conceived by the temple that spring night escaped abandonment in the woods some midwinter night.

But the thralls didn't need to know how poorly Ausi had behaved after she had drunk beer and witnessed the priests of fornication.

The days had grown longer, and the blanket of snow dazzled the eyes. But the ice was still thick when the thralls saw a sled approaching from the north with three or four people on it. It turned toward the settlement, and the onlookers saw a little boy trying to take the reins from the driver. Beside him sat a woman with fair hair under her cap.

As they got closer, everyone recognized the woman and child. It was the chieftain's wife and son, but beside her sat a blond-bearded stranger. When he stepped out of the sled, the thralls could see he was as tall and thin as the dead chieftain had been short and stout. They all suspected he was the new lord.

The chieftain's wife had changed entirely. In a gruff voice, she told the thralls that the good days were over now. She was furious that they had moved into the high hall and set up house inside. Everyone had to move either down by the door or into the thrall dwellings immediately.

She looked at Ausi and Holme strangely and talked softly with her new husband, who nodded meekly to everything she said and then approached Holme. In an indifferent voice, he ordered him and his woman to leave before the next day and never show themselves again. Holme had been defiant and had played the lord long enough. Besides, he had injured the child over there; he'd never be like other children.

Stor and Tan regained their authority as foremen and looked triumphantly at Holme and Ausi. But it was no broken-hearted Holme who walked to the smithy to gather up his belongings. He had anticipated a hasty end to his chieftainship and was just as glad for a change from the monotonous life at the settlement.

The chieftain's wife, who had expected resistance and defiance from Holme, forgot her old fear of him. This might be her chance to be revenged for the rock he had thrown from the forest. In the afternoon when the thralls were ready to depart with their burdens, she walked up to them, followed by her obliging husband stroking his blond beard. The little dark girl, now as clean and well-clothed as a chieftain's child, was standing between Holme and Ausi.

'She stays here,' the woman ordered, pointing at the child. 'My son will need thralls when he gets bigger.'

Her husband nodded assent. Beside them, the group of thralls stood in tense and silent expectation. Stor and Tan were smiling maliciously at the front of the group.

Before Holme fully grasped her meaning, it became so quiet everyone could hear a dog crunching a bone on the refuse pile. Feeling rage surge to his head, Holme scanned the crowd before him to see if anyone was on his side. Only Stor and Tan supported the chieftain's wife, and Holme wasn't afraid of them. His helpers let him know with a wink where they stood.

Holme told Ausi to go on with the child; he picked up his bundle in his left hand and his ax in his right. The chieftain's wife repeated her order, but her voice had lost its authority. Holme, glancing back over his shoulder, saw her stop her spider of a husband from coming after him with his sword. But Stor and Tan were ordered, as before, to take the child from them. They followed hesitantly on the forest path, and Holme laughed loudly and scornfully, his woman and child walking before him.

Ausi hadn't really felt afraid the whole time. She knew no one at the settlement would dare tangle with Holme. But they had a long and hard road ahead of them. They were warmly dressed and had plenty of food, but it was still winter. She had heard the wolves howling one night not too long ago. The protracted, desolate howling had forced its way in through the smoke vent, and she hadn't been able to fall asleep for a long time afterward.

They weren't at a loss about where to go this time. Holme would probably be welcome at the smithy, and the hut still suited them. Their only regret was leaving the boat Holme had built, but the ice hadn't broken up yet.

The first day's journey was the most difficult because there was no road to follow in the snow. Toward nightfall, they took turns carrying the child, who couldn't stay awake any longer. The weather was mild, and they could rest wherever they wanted, on a rock or a tree blown over by the wind. They had long since passed the cave; it was only a short day's walk away, and it no longer enticed them as it had before, with all that had happened at the time of the winter sacrifice.

It was late when they reached a farmstead and went into an outlying building. A few emaciated cows were standing around, and the moon was shining in through the ceiling hole. Holme found some dry grass for a bed and then went out with a wooden bucket to find water. Ausi had eaten snow the whole night. He soon found the well's black circle in the snow, and after a meal of meat, bread, and water, all three slept heavily until dawn. They didn't see anyone at the farmstead when they walked on.

Three days later, toward nightfall, they were at the lake. A broad road, dark with horse droppings, led toward the town. There were deep tracks after the midday thaw, but the water had frozen crisp on the surface, and they saw only a few people on foot.

They headed off the road toward the forest where they had lived before. It was just as well not to pass through town. Holme thought now and then about what had happened when he had gotten their child back. He might have hit the woman a little too hard, but he didn't think she had died. He probably had nothing to fear after such a long time. At the worst, he might have to give her something in recompense.

Not until they were standing in front of the hut did they see the faint smoke rising through the hole in the roof and a narrow path leading up to the door. They hadn't once suspected that it might be occupied while they were away. Ausi looked with fatigue and despair at Holme. The surprise on his face changed to ferocity before her eyes. He was tired too and had looked forward to a fire, some food, and rest.

Holme put his burden down and picked up his ax. Then he walked up and knocked on the door. It was opened immediately by a middle-aged man also holding an ax.

The man stared with surprise at the man and woman looking at him with wild hatred in their eyes. He didn't know them and couldn't have done them any harm.

'Get out,' Holme growled through clenched teeth.

The man answered that he had lived there the whole winter and had a right to stay. They could find another empty hut.

He didn't get to finish talking and didn't have time to raise his own ax more than halfway. There was no sound except the ax blow and the soft thud when the man hit the floor. Immediately Holme grabbed him and dragged him out into the woods.

Ausi went inside, grateful for the warmth. Their old skin rugs were still there, but there were some new things too. She laid the sleeping child on the bench, went out for some snow, and sprinkled it over the blood on the floor. The man had gathered up a big pile of firewood, so Holme wouldn't have to go out into the woods for several days.

They said nothing about the man when Holme returned, but lay down to sleep on the familiar benches. He was undoubtedly an outlaw no one would miss.

Spring found the king at one of his farmsteads, taking counsel with his top men. Trade with the Christian lands had fallen off and they were afraid it might stop altogether. There was much that they needed from other lands.

Several envoys had returned with the message that trade would increase if the northern people would receive those men wanting to spread the new teaching, if they would protect their lives, and let them build a church.

The king talked it over with his men, and they decided to meet the Christians' demands. The foreign priests would be allowed to come; they'd see to it they didn't do any great harm.

New envoys boarded ship, and the king carefully instructed them which goods were needed most and first. He gave them a special token so that everyone would recognize them as his envoys and would give them safe passage.[25]

That summer at the settlement, sparse blades of grass began to sprout on the chieftain's mound. The chieftain's wife reigned and his bull-necked son ran loose. His light-bearded successor walked around in an ineffectual daze; all he had to do was take care of the sacrifices. The high hall remained empty and cold unless relatives came to visit.

In the town's largest smithy, Holme had become the master smith. His predecessor had drowned on a fishing trip. Holme, Ausi, and the girl now lived inside the town walls.

The stranger's bones whitened along with the others. Many remembered him and his words, but only two remembered with

25. The Swedish king is Björn, the Christian king, Louis the Pious (788–840), son of Charlemagne and emperor of the Holy Roman Empire 814–40.

hunger and sorrow in their hearts. One was the old warrior; the other was Ausi. She was still waiting; the stranger wasn't, he couldn't be, gone forever. Surely some day, he would either come himself or send a message.

Far to the south in the Christian land, new men were equipping vessels to sail to the Norsemen with the light.

Afterword

They dominated most of the known world from the eighth to the eleventh century, earning themselves such descriptions as 'wolves from the sea,' devising such extraordinary barbarities as 'the blood eagle,' a particularly savage form of execution in which they cut the condemned man's ribs away from his spine and pulled his lungs out to form bloody wings on his back. Legend tells us that King Ella of Northumbria suffered this death at the hands of the Dane Ragnar Loðbrok in 867.[1] Other individuals, indeed whole cities, from Hamburg to Chartres to Dublin, likewise fell victim to the Viking raids. But while they had dire reputations as fierce pirates, the Vikings also created art and literature of rare force and beauty. They lost their piratical edge on the high seas with the advent of ships like the galley, hulk, and cog, which were much higher and less assailable in the water than the long ships, and for that and other reasons their way of life eventually died.[2] As they disappeared into history, however, the memory of their ferocity and the evidence of their literary and artistic skills retained their grip on the imagination of western Europe and America.

Their literature, austere, mysterious, 'masculine' in the extreme, has been a major source of inspiration. Particularly influential are the Eddic and Scaldic poems, the Old Icelandic sagas, and Saxo Grammaticus's *Gesta Danorum,* together with the Old English poem *Beowulf.* In English and American literature we find Viking themes and stories manifesting themselves in a wide range of works, ranging from those of Thomas Gray (1716–71), Robert Southey (1774–1843), William Morris (1834–96), and J. R. R. Tolkien (1892–1973) on one side of the Atlantic, to those of John Greenleaf Whittier (1807–92), Henry Wadsworth Longfellow (1807–82), Jack London (1876–1916), and Michael Crichton (b. 1942) on the other. In Scandinavian literature the Vikings understandably have a particularly strong foothold, their world appearing in a relatively unbroken line in works from such authors as Esaias Tegnér (1782–1846), Erik Gustaf Geijer (1783–1847), Adam Oehlenschläger (1779–1850), and Johan Ludwig Runeberg (1804–77), to Henrik Ibsen (1828–1906), Frans G. Bengtsson (1894–1954), Vilhelm Moberg (1898–1973), Halldór Laxness (b. 1902), and Villy Sørensen (b. 1929).[3] The early writers naturally engage in romanticizing and idealizing the Viking warrior, turning him into a symbol of Scandinavian purity and strength, while later writers tend to take a much more skeptical, sometimes ironic, view. For Tegnér, the Viking was a civilized, noble seafarer, but for Laxness, he was a grotesque parody of a true hero.[4]

When Jan Fridegård (1897–1968), an influential modern pro-
letarian author, began writing about the Vikings, then, he was
working within an established tradition, even as he intended not to
praise the Vikings but to use them as a medium for social criticism.[5] His *Land of Wooden Gods*, the first novel of a trilogy about
Holme, also fits within a subgroup of that critical tradition, the
group focused on Viking thralls. Three Nobel Prize winners writing before Fridegård, for instance, the Dane Karl Gjellerup
(1857–1919), the Swede Selma Lagerlöf (1858–1940), and the
Norwegian Sigrid Undset (1882–1949), treat thralls sympathet-
ically; and strictly within Swedish literature Fredrika Bremer
(1801–65), Viktor Rydberg (1828–95), Verner von Heidenstam
(1859–1940), and Gustaf Fröding (1860–1911) all show varying de-
grees of compassion for the Viking slave. Bremer does so in her
play about oppression and hatred, *The Slave Girl* (*Trälinnan*, 1840),
Rydberg in his attack on industrialism in his poem 'The New Song
of Grotti' ('Den nya Grottesången,' 1891), a reworking of the Old
Norse *Grottasǫngr*, Heidenstam in his mildly critical depiction of
slavery in his novel about eleventh-century Sweden, *The Tree of the
Folkungs* (*Folkungaträdet*, 1905, 1907), and Fröding in his radical re-
interpretation of the Old Norse legend of Weyland in his poem
'The Smith' ('Smeden,' 1892), which I will discuss below. No one
before Fridegård, however, concentrated so much interest on the
Viking thralls and what he felt had to be their inevitable fight for
freedom.[6]

Fridegård had little evidence for substantiating his portrayal of
Viking slavery, just a brief study or two by some of his contempor-
aries, and so most of the story and much of the milieu in the
Holme trilogy Fridegård created himself.[7] The backdrop for Fridegård's anti-ideal saga basically develops out of three different
kinds of sources: archeological descriptions of the Viking period,

such as a Norwegian museum catalog and reports about excavation sites; cultural studies, such as a 1938 work on Nordic religion and Christianity; and a ninth-century saint's life chronicling the career of Ansgar, the archbishop of Hamburg who conducted the first recorded mission to Sweden in ca. A.D. 830.[8] The first kind of source allows Fridegård to create a believable atmosphere for which he has often been praised.[9] From descriptions of buildings to agricultural techniques and burial practices, Fridegård has been fairly precise, making only occasional and understandable errors as when he refers to horned helmets, which Vikings never actually wore. To ensure the right historical flavor, Fridegård even takes the names of all his characters from rune stones in the Uppland area of Sweden and keeps both dialogue and the use of archaisms to a minimum, since either device could easily make the novels sound false.[10] The second kind of source material, cultural studies, enables Fridegård to establish a primitivistic or naturalistic atmosphere that he felt was important for a period not yet fully restricted by the Christian antipathy to sexuality. For example, he draws heavily on Helge Ljungberg's *Nordic Religion and Christianity: Studies in the Nordic Religious Shift during the Viking Period,* which provides a thorough analysis of the pagan temple at Uppsala and the nine-day festival of sacrifice that used to take place there. In creating a primitivistic atmosphere, Fridegård aligns himself with authors such as Sherwood Anderson (1876–1941), whose *Dark Laughter* (1925) he greatly admired, and D. H. Lawrence (1885–1930), whose *The Plumed Serpent* (1926) may have influenced his erotic descriptions in *Land of Wooden Gods* (1940) and *Sacrificial Smoke (Offerök,* 1949), the last volume in the trilogy. Fridegård's 'primitivism' in these novels further augments their sense of historical accuracy and verisimilitude since the books describe a past era and sensibility.

The third source that Fridegård used in writing his trilogy is Bishop Rimbert's *Vita Anskarii* (*The Life of Ansgar*), and this source, unlike the other two, he modifies for his own purposes.[12] While he frequently follows Rimbert quite closely, he just as frequently deviates severely from the *vita*. Some of his inaccuracies may have been inadvertent, such as his anachronistic depiction of Christ as a frail, effeminate godhead, an image that was the product of the late, not early, Middle Ages.[13] But others clearly are not casual mistakes. Ansgar, for example, did not neglect the poor, as Fridegård implies throughout *People of the Dawn* (*Gryningsfolket*, 1944) and *Sacrificial Smoke*, but instead founded a hospital for them in Bremen and 'gave away for the support of the poor a tenth of the animals and of all his revenues and a tenth of the tithes which belonged to him, and whatever money or property of any kind came to him he gave a tenth for the benefit of the poor.' Neither would Ansgar have countenanced the kind of lust for money that Fridegård's priests display, especially in *Sacrificial Smoke*. Rimbert tells us that Ansgar gave strict orders to missionaries 'that they should not desire nor seek to obtain the property of anyone' but rather 'be content with food and raiment.'[14] And finally, Fridegård's implication that Christianity exacerbated the problem of slavery instead of solving it does not bear scrutiny. Modern historians, in fact, tell us precisely the opposite.[15] Fridegård has obviously made deliberate changes in Rimbert's account of the period for a political agenda that is anarchist in origin and demands a rereading of history. Since little recorded history actually exists for slaves, and none for the rebellions they raise in the trilogy, Fridegård creates a story fabricated in many particulars, but based on a socialist understanding of the processes of history and, from his point of view, therefore true in its essential outline: oppressed people necessarily rebel against their oppressors.[16] As an anti-ideal designed to undermine a political and literary image of Sweden's past, which venerates the Viking and ignores the thrall, the Holme trilogy remakes Nordic history to create a new ethos.[17] In Fridegård's new myth, Holme functions centrally as a representative of the rising proletariat in Sweden, and the interconnections Fridegård establishes between Holme and the other characters in the novels become of paramount importance.[18] They are the focus of Fridegård's higher purpose of reinterpreting history through anarchist ideology and are what make the trilogy a serious work of social and philosophical criticism.

To understand how Fridegård uses Holme to advance his cause, we must look closely at Gustaf Fröding's 'The Smith,' a poem that greatly impressed Fridegård.[19] In forty-eight lines, Fröding recreates the Old Norse legend of Weyland (Völundr), the king of the elves and a skillful smith, who, along with his prize sword, was captured by the Swedish king Níðuðr. Níðuðr, wanting to take advantage of Weyland's skills, had Weyland's hamstrings cut so he couldn't escape and then isolated him on an island where he had to make treasures for Níðuðr. When Níðuðr's two sons came to see Weyland work, he cut off their heads and made their skulls into silver vessels for Níðuðr, their eyes into jewels for Níðuðr's wife, and their teeth into a necklace for Níðuðr's daughter. Through artifice, a laughing Weyland then raised himself aloft and out of reach.[20]

In his rendition, Fröding dispenses with the specifics of the Weyland story, focusing instead on the idea of the smith's rebellion against his oppressors. The poem opens with the poet dreaming he is walking through a coal-black forest with treetops like iron and a wind that causes the surroundings to quake, not whisper. The path he walks on is strewn with soot, not covered with grass, and there he hears one noise that sounds like people tramping heavily and another that resembles the muffled sound of a sword clashing against a dagger. As he dreams, the poet discovers that he is near Weyland's valley and that the sound he hears carries the warning of impending storm 'and the feud of the mighty powers' ('och de väldiga makternas fejd'). When he hears the clanging of a hammer and sees sparks rising, he moves forward to investigate, but all he finds is a scraggly, hunched-over, disheveled smith, with low forehead and crooked back, a mere thrall laborer, 'one of the thralls who live in the cellars / beneath the overlord's tramping heels' ('en av trälarnes folk, som i källrar bo / under herrarnes trampande häl'). The poet thinks the man is a modern, harmless smith. But then the smith rises, becoming tall, noble, and straight. His mighty arm strikes with its tool at the smithy's iron roof, 'and heavy as a mountain the hammer fell / and like thunder was the roar of the blow' ('och tungt som ett fjäll föll hammarens slag / och som åskan var slagets dån'). Weyland has been a thrall smith for a thousand years, says the poet, but now he fashions the sword of revenge that will destroy the dwelling of the gods. The dreamer then realizes that the forest is actually a modern factory that will one day feel the force of Weyland's revolt. It, like the forest, is filled with a noise like the clashing of sword against dagger, and soot covers its walls and roof as well.[21]

Fröding transforms the thrall smith in the course of the poem in three specific ways, all of which have importance for Fridegård's Holme trilogy: first, he changes the bent and scraggly thrall smith into a massive, noble figure; second, he turns the nameless, insignificant, unattractive slave into the legendary Weyland, who is capable of leading a revolution; and third, after changing the smith into Weyland, he also conflates Weyland with the Nordic god

Thor, whose hammer makes thunder and protects gods and men from their enemies. Fridegård uses the same pattern of transformation in depicting Holme.

Holme's transformations into a noble figure and into a figure capable of leading a revolution are easy to apprehend. Although Holme is never bent and scraggly, he does crouch in *Land of Wooden Gods* as an animal would (pp. 6, 10, 13) and is even likened there to various animals (e.g., an owl, p. 9; a dog, p. 30; a wild animal, p. 153), as well as to a subhuman shadow (p. 10) and ghost (p. 13). He also has wide cheekbones (p. 6), reminiscent of Fröding's smith's low forehead, and has a primitive, animallike walk (p. 70). After he has established himself as a respected smith in Birka, however, such imagery rarely occurs.[22] A change in Holme's relationship to his antagonists coincides with the disappearance of animal imagery. His stature, strength, and capabilities become magnified as the trilogy progresses, and he, like Weyland, becomes larger than life. While we cannot know that he could have beaten Stenulf in *Land of Wooden Gods,* for instance, we never have any doubt that he will vanquish Geire, his primary opponent in *People of the Dawn,* and any other opponent in *Sacrificial Smoke.* Further, the relatively selfish Holme who raped Ausi before the trilogy begins (p. 20), who in *Land of the Wooden Gods* saves his own child from certain death but who puts Ausi's child by another man out in the forest to die (p. 186), and who kills a man rightfully inhabiting a house that once was his (p. 192), becomes the Holme who neglects his own needs to save the starving thralls in *People of the Dawn,* and who has a vision of freedom, without violence, for all mankind in *Sacrificial Smoke.* The transformation that begins within Holme eventually has ramifications for all around him as he becomes a revolutionary leader.

The third transformation of Holme, into a kind of Thor figure, is by far the most complex. It develops simultaneously with the other two, beginning, curiously enough, with the stranger in *Land of Wooden Gods,* and ending with the conflation of Holme, the stranger, Christ, and Thor by the end of the trilogy. The stranger, first of all, represents a primitive, 'socialist' kind of Christianity that is egalitarian, nonmaterialistic, and dedicated to converting society from the bottom up.[23] The stranger begins with the thralls, going 'down among the workers and the overburdened' as Christ once did (p. 76). This socialist ideal has an obvious affinity with what Holme later develops in the trilogy, for he too works for an egalitarian society beginning with the thralls. Other aspects of the stranger's character and description, however, tie him still more closely to Holme. Both he and Holme, for example, come from distant lands, which makes them somewhat mysterious (pp. 19, 60); both seem to some to be sorcerers (pp. 19, 60, 68); both have striking eyes (e.g., pp. 68, 74; pp. 11, 24, 30); and both have a powerful effect on Ausi, who perceives another similarity in both *People of the Dawn* and *Sacrificial Smoke.* The stranger, she muses, 'must have been closer to Christ than those who came after him' and Holme, too, 'was a lot like Christ' in helping the poor and defending the weak. Holme probably would not have appreciated the comparison, but Ausi makes it nonetheless and solidifies Holme's identification with Christ and the stranger as the trilogy develops. In *People of the Dawn,* for instance, the stranger actually becomes Christ, Christ and Holme both live within Ausi, and she belongs to both. In addition, Ausi observes that all three men are persecuted and eventually die for their revolutionary faiths.

Holme's faith partakes of more than the primitive Christianity represented by the stranger. It partakes, as well, of the Nordic religion as represented by Thor. Here again, Fridegård takes liberties with his sources in order to advance his view of history as he transposes his paradigm for Christianity's development – from egalitarian to elitist – onto Nordic paganism. We have no evidence, after all, that the Norse gods were undemocratic in bestowing their favors on their subjects, as Fridegård says they were (e.g., p. 86). Instead we have considerable proof that Thor was the god of common men and peasants, perhaps even thralls.[24] He was, in fact, more like the Weyland/Thor figure in Fröding's poem than the battle god in the trilogy, and Fridegård fashions Holme in the Fröding mold in distinct, though subtle ways.

Fridegård first creates a broad and loose association between the god and Holme by making the latter a smith as well as a thrall. Thor was the patron of smiths, a fact that may account for the otherwise curious transformation that Weyland undergoes in Fröding's poem, and the thralls' weapon and tool, the ax, was almost as strongly associated with Thor as his hammer was. That Holme actually uses both the hammer and ax in battle brings an even closer association between him and Thor. The silver amulets representing Thor's hammer may have been made in conscious opposition to symbols of the cross, and Holme uses his hammer at least twice against Christian symbols, when he destroys the baptismal font and the bell tower in *People of the Dawn*. His hammer, it seems, becomes Thor's, and his acts also reflect those of the god, to whom men turned for protection from Christ. Furthermore, consciously or not, Fridegård draws the parallel between Holme and Thor still tighter by alluding to Holme's intimidating power. In legend, Thor challenges Christ to a battle, but Christ backs down before Thor's superior might.[25] In *People of the Dawn*, Ausi recognizes that Holme renders all gods, 'both the old ones and the new one' powerless. Finally, in *Land of Wooden Gods*, Fridegård likens Holme to a wooden god (p. 171) and in *Sacrificial Smoke* places him in Thor's traditional spot in the middle of the heathen temple during the final confrontation with the Christians.

Holme, of course, never fully becomes Thor, just as he never fully becomes Christ. His life is far too rooted in a socioeconomic, rather than a religious or spiritual, reality for him to be either. Instead, he rises up a noble, straight-backed, and clear-sighted man, with his thoughts fixed on the welfare of his fellows. His ultimate vision, then, fleetingly realized through Ausi's eyes in her dying moments, is not that of the destruction coming with a Ragnarok or Armageddon but of the creation of a just and different world. That vision gives him his strength and stature, and the new myth that Fridegård creates through Holme thus proceeds not from a godhead, Christian or pagan, but from an idea – that to all mankind belong freedom and equality. Fridegård has rewritten myth in his Holme trilogy to give the proletariat a history and a hope. In the distant past, in the beginnings of Scandinavian society, lie the beginnings of a better future.

Notes

1. Gwyn Jones, *A History of the Vikings*, revised ed. (Oxford: Oxford Univ. Press, 1984), p. 219.

2. Magnus Magnusson, 'End of an Era,' *Scandinavian Review* 68, no. 3. (1980): 60. On the collapse of the Viking world, see Jones, *History of the Vikings*. Jones's is the standard history of the period.

3. On the use of Viking motifs in European and North and South American literature, see Jöran Mjöberg, 'Romanticism and Revival' in David M. Wilson, ed. *The Northern World: The History and Heritage of Northern Europe* AD 400–1100 (New York: Harry N. Abrams, 1980), pp. 207–38. Mjöberg's *Drömmen om sagatiden*, 2 vols. (Stockholm: Natur och kultur, 1967–68) is the definitive work on the subject.

4. See Tegnér's *Frithiof's Saga*, trans. Ida Mauch (New York: Exposition Press, 1960) and Laxness's novel *The Happy Warriors* (*Gerpla*, 1952), trans. Katherine John

(London: Methuen, 1958). See also Runeberg's epic poem *King Fialar: A Poem in Five Songs* (*King Fjalar*, 1844), trans. Eiríkr Magnússon (London: J. M. Dent & Sons, Ltd., 1912). And for a classic Viking novel, see Bengtsson's justly famous *The Long Ships: A Saga of the Viking Age* (*Röde Orm*, 1941, 1945), trans. Michael Meyer (1954; rpt. New York and London: Collins, 1986).

5. Jan Fridegård (1897–1968) was born into a poor working-class family of seven in Enköpings-Näs, an area in central Sweden just north of Lake Mälar. His father was a *statare*, a farm laborer tied to a large estate and earning his wages partly in cash but mostly in kind (*stat*). The brutal statare system, which arose in the eighteenth century to support the aristocratic estates and survived until 1945, almost guaranteed illiteracy and social immobility in its victims and has a pervasive role in Fridegård's work. Of his close to thirty novels and his numerous short stories and essays, most are autobiographical, depicting the lives of lower-class working people. The thralls in *Land of Wooden Gods* seem clearly to represent the oppressed statare.

6. Nobel Prize winners: e.g., Gjellerup's plays, *Brynhild* (1884) and *Kong Hjarne Skald* (1893) and Lagerlöf's stories 'The Legend of Reor' ('Reors saga,' 1893) in *Invisible Links*, trans. Pauline Bancroft Flach (Garden City, N.Y.: Doubleday, Page, 1899) and 'Astrid' (1899) in *The Queens of Kungahälla and Other Sketches* (*Drottningar i Kungahälla*, 1899), trans. Claud Field (London: T. W. Laurie 1917). On these works and Undset, see Mjöberg, *Drömmen om sagatiden*, vol. 2, pp. 285–86, 452ff. Bremer: in *The H—Family: Trälinnan: Axel and Anna and Other Tales*, trans. Mary Howitt, 2 vols. (London: Longman, Brown, Green, and Långemans, 1844). Rydberg: see Wilson, *Northern World*, p. 234. Heidenstam: trans. A. G. Chater (New York: A. A. Knopf, 1925). On the Viking slave motif in Scandinavian literature, see Mjöberg, *Drömmen om sagatiden*, vol. 2, pp. 285–90.

7. Ebbe Schön, *Jan Fridegård och forntiden. En studie i diktverk och källor* (Uppsala, Sweden: Almqvist & Wiksell, 1973), pp. 61ff., discusses some of the popular works on Viking slavery that Fridegård may have read. For a recent discussion of thralls in the Viking period, see Peter G. Foote and David M. Wilson, *The Viking Achievement: A Survey of the Society and Culture of Early Medieval Scandinavia* (New York: Praeger, 1970), pp. 65–78.

8. Schön, *Fridegård och forntiden*, pp. 23–153, offers a thorough analysis of Fridegård's sources.

9. See, for example, Erik Hjalmar Linder, *Fem decennier av nittonhundratalet*, 4th ed. [vol. 2 of *Ny illustrerad svensk litteraturhistoria*] (Stockholm: Natur och kultur, 1966), pp. 589–90.

10. Schön, *Fridegård och forntiden*, pp. 152–53; pp. 30, 52.

11. Helge Ljungberg, *Den nordiska religionen och kristendomen. Studier över det nordiska religionsskiftet under vikingatiden* (Stockholm: Hugo Gebers förlag, 1938); Schön, *Fridegård och forntiden*, pp. 95 and 113.

12. For an English translation, see Charles H. Robinson, *Anskar: Apostle of the North*, 801–865 (London: Society for the Propagation of the Gospel in Foreign Parts, 1921).

13. On Christ as Germanic hero, see Ljungberg, *Den nordiska religionen och kristendomen*, p. 95; Axel Olrik, *Viking Civilization* (1930; rpt. New York: Norton, 1971), pp. 141ff.; and chapter 8 ('Christ as Poetic Hero') in Stanley B. Greenfield and Daniel G. Calder, *A New Critical History of Old English Literature* (New York: New York Univ. Press, 1986).

14. *Anskar*, chapter 35, p. 112; chapter 33, pp. 104–5.

15. See, for example, Foote and Wilson, *Viking Achievement*, pp. 77ff.

16. Schön, *Fridegård och forntiden*, pp. 61–79.

17. Schön, *Fridegård och forntiden*, p. 51, says that Fridegård sometimes wrote in conscious opposition to Tegnér's *Frithiof's Saga*.

18. Schön (*Fridegård och forntiden*, p. 28) observes that the story about Holme 'is to a certain extent to be regarded as a kind of social myth where Fridegård, with the help of his imagination, tries to explain the origin of the struggle of the proletariat' in Sweden.

19. Schön, *Fridegård och forntiden*, p. 50. Mjöberg, *Drömmen om sagatiden*, 2, pp. 291–92, asserts, but does not really show, the importance of Fröding's poem to Fridegård's trilogy.

20. For a translation of 'The Lay of Völundr' or 'Weyland,' see D. G. Calder, R. E. Bjork, P. K. Ford, D. F. Melia, *Sources and Analogues of Old English Poetry II: The Major Germanic and Celtic Texts in Translation* (Cambridge: D. S. Brewer, 1983), pp. 65–69.

21. Gustaf Fröding, *Dikter*, Magnus von Platen, ed. (Stockholm: Bokförlaget Prisma, 1962), pp. 297–98.

22. Animal imagery recurs when Holme is back at the settlement or fleeing from his persecutors in *Sacrificial Smoke* (i.e, 'pig,' 'night animal,' 'wolf' and 'fox'). He is also compared to a troll on one occasion.

23. See Ljungberg, *Den nordiska religionen och kristendomen*, pp. 77ff., and Schön, *Fridegård och forntiden*, pp. 124–25.

24. See E. O. G. Turville-Petre's chapter on Thor in *Myth and Religion of the North* (New York: Holt, Rinehart, and Winston, 1964), pp. 75–105.

25. Turville-Petre, *Myth and Religion*, p. 84; p. 90.

Selected Bibliography

Translations

Fridegård, Jan. *I, Lars Hård (Jag Lars Hård,* 1935). Translated, with introduction and notes, by Robert E. Bjork. Lincoln: Univ. of Nebraska Press, 1983.

—. Jacob's Ladder (*Tack för himlastegen,* 1936) and *Mercy (Barmhärtighet,* 1936). Translated, with introductions and notes, by Robert E. Bjork. Lincoln: Univ. of Nebraska Press, 1985.

—. 'The Key' ('Nyckeln,' 1944). Translated by Robert E. Bjork. *Translation: The Journal of Literary Translation* 15 (1985): 270–75.

—. 'Natural Selection' ('Det naturliga urvalet,' 1939). Translated by Robert E. Bjork. *Malahat Review* 55 (1980): 104–10.

—. '100 Kilos Rye' ('Kvarnbudet,' 1944). translated by Robert E. Bjork. *Scandinavian Review* 68, no. 2 (1980): 54–62.

—. '1987 Translation Prize Selection from *Land of Wooden Gods.*'
Translated by Robert E. Bjork, *Scandinavian Review* 76, no. 4
(1988): 77–82.

Criticism

Gamby, Erik. *Jan Fridegård. Introduktion till ett författarskap.* Stockholm: Svenska bokförlaget, 1956.

Graves, Peter. *Jan Fridegård: Lars Hård.* Studies in Swedish Literature, no. 8. Hull: University of Hull, 1977. (In English.)

Lundkvist, Artur, and Lars Forssell, eds. *Jan Fridegård.* Stockholm: Förlaget frilansen, 1949.

Schön, Ebbe. *Jan Fridegård och forntiden. En studie i diktverk och
källor.* Uppsala: Almqvist & Wiksell, 1973.

—. *Jan Fridegård. Proletärdiktaren och folkkulturen.* Stockholm:
Wahlstrom & Widstrand, 1978.